D0532113

Body Image

by Ronald D. Lankford Jr.

BIBLIOTHÈQUE SAINT-CLAUDE LIBRARY
C. P. 203
SAINT-CLAUDE, MANITOBA   R0G 1Z0   379-2524

LUCENT BOOKS
A part of Gale, Cengage Learning

Detroit • New York • San Francisco • New Haven, Conn • Waterville, Maine • London

© 2010 Gale, Cengage Learning

ALL RIGHTS RESERVED. No part of this work covered by the copyright herein may be reproduced, transmitted, stored, or used in any form or by any means graphic, electronic, or mechanical, including but not limited to photocopying, recording, scanning, digitizing, taping, Web distribution, information networks, or information storage and retrieval systems, except as permitted under Section 107 or 108 of the 1976 United States Copyright Act, without the prior written permission of the publisher.

Every effort has been made to trace the owners of copyrighted material.

LIBRARY OF CONGRESS CATALOGING-IN-PUBLICATION DATA

Lankford, Ronald D., 1962-
  Body image / by Ronald D. Lankford Jr.
    p. cm. -- (Hot topics)
  Includes bibliographical references and index.
  ISBN 978-1-4205-0146-9 (hardcover)
  1. Body image. I. Title.
  BF697.5.B63L36 2010
  306.4'613--dc22

                                        2009024472

Lucent Books
27500 Drake Rd.
Farmington Hills, MI 48331

ISBN-13: 978-1-4205-0146-9
ISBN-10: 1-4205-0146-1

Printed in the United States of America
1 2 3 4 5 6 7 14 13 12 11 10
Printed by Bang Printing, Brainerd, MN, 1st Ptg., 05/2010

CONTENTS

DO NOT TAPE OR REPAIR LIBRARY BOOKS

FOREWORD

Young people today are bombarded with information. Aside from traditional sources such as newspapers, television, and the radio, they are inundated with a nearly continuous stream of data from electronic media. They send and receive e-mails and instant messages, read and write online "blogs," participate in chat rooms and forums, and surf the Web for hours. This trend is likely to continue. As Patricia Senn Breivik, the former dean of university libraries at Wayne State University in Detroit, has stated, "Information overload will only increase in the future. By 2020, for example, the available body of information is expected to double every 73 days! How will these students find the information they need in this coming tidal wave of information?"

Ironically, this overabundance of information can actually impede efforts to understand complex issues. Whether the topic is abortion, the death penalty, gay rights, or obesity, the deluge of fact and opinion that floods the print and electronic media is overwhelming. The news media report the results of polls and studies that contradict one another. Cable news shows, talk radio programs, and newspaper editorials promote narrow viewpoints and omit facts that challenge their own political biases. The World Wide Web is an electronic minefield where legitimate scholars compete with the postings of ordinary citizens who may or may not be well-informed or capable of reasoned argument. At times, strongly worded testimonials and opinion pieces both in print and electronic media are presented as factual accounts.

Conflicting quotes and statistics can confuse even the most diligent researchers. A good example of this is the question of whether or not the death penalty deters crime. For instance, one study found that murders decreased by nearly one-third when the death penalty was reinstated in New York in 1995. Death penalty supporters cite this finding to support their argument that the existence of the death penalty deters criminals from committing murder. However, another study found that states without the death penalty have murder rates below the national average. This study is cited by opponents of capital punishment, who reject the claim that the death penalty deters murder. Students need context and clear, informed discussion if they are to think critically and make informed decisions.

The Hot Topics series is designed to help young people wade through the glut of fact, opinion, and rhetoric so that they can think critically about controversial issues. Only by reading and thinking critically will they be able to formulate a viewpoint that is not simply the parroted views of others. Each volume of the series focuses on one of today's most pressing social issues and provides a balanced overview of the topic. Carefully crafted narrative, fully documented primary and secondary source quotes, informative sidebars, and study questions all provide excellent starting points for research and discussion. Full-color photographs and charts enhance all volumes in the series. With its many useful features, the Hot Topics series is a valuable resource for young people struggling to understand the pressing issues of the modern era.

INTRODUCTION

APPEARANCE
OBSESSION

Since the early 1980s, body image has been at the center of public debate, generating much discussion and, at times, controversy. Simply defined, body image is the concept that each individual forms about his or her own appearance. In the public realm, however, ideas about body image have splintered into a broad array of issues with personal, social, and political implications. Weight, for instance, has become a hot-button issue. How thin is too thin, how heavy is "obese," and how are these standards decided? Body image, then, is not just an abstract concept that one reads about in books but a reality that affects people's everyday lives.

Issues surrounding body image include dieting, weight lifting, and eating disorders. Dieting has become a multibillion-dollar industry in the United States and around the world, as men and women attempt to achieve and maintain an ideal body weight. Likewise, membership in gyms and health clubs has become increasingly popular. Many people, however, have relied on more extreme methods to control their body shapes. While statistics on eating disorders are difficult to verify, many researchers believe that anorexia, bulimia, and binge eating are all on the rise. Furthermore, while these diseases have been traditionally associated with women, men have begun developing these disorders in greater numbers. Researchers are also increasingly concerned that while women may wish to become thinner, many men wish to become more muscular. In some cases this has led to exercise addiction and steroid abuse.

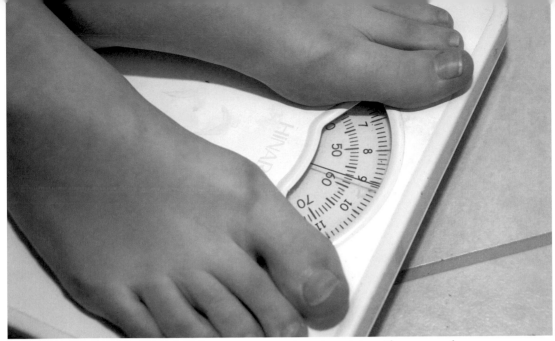

Body image issues have become very prominent in society, with more people dieting, bodybuilding, and having cosmetic procedures.

Other body image issues have also become more prevalent, including decorating and physically altering the body. Pierced ears, for instance, allow individuals to enhance that part of their bodies, potentially enhancing their overall body images. During the 1970s body piercings and tattoos were frequently associated with social subgroups such as punk rockers. Body jewelry helped to identify individuals as members of the punk community, working as a social shortcut while also separating them from the mainstream. Today, piercings have become more fashionable, perhaps serving as a sign of fitting in rather than of exclusion. Likewise, cosmetic surgery has become much more common, with millions of men and women receiving liposuction, Botox injections, and face-lifts every year. These changes suggest that men and women today have become more focused on body image issues and that it has become socially acceptable to alter or decorate the body in order to enhance one's body image.

Researchers believe that a number of factors, including genes, family, peers, the media, and advertising, influence the development of body image. Research also suggests that a number of other factors, including gender and age, also affect how men and women think about body image issues. The development of body

Decorating the body with piercings and tattoos has become more accepted and mainstream.

image, then, is a complex issue and one that researchers will continue to study closely.

Because body image has become a much-discussed and much-debated issue, some observers have suggested that it has become an obsession. This is reflected in a number of studies in

Western cultures that suggest that body image is the single most important factor in a person's overall self-image. Whereas body image is focused on physical appearance, self-image is a broader concept that includes an individual's image of his or her overall personality. By weighing body image so heavily, a woman who considers herself attractive will have both a positive body image and a positive self-image. While most people wish to be considered attractive, hyper-focus on body image may ignore many other aspects of an individual's personality. Whether or not one agrees that men and women have become hyper-focused on body image in contemporary culture, the issues that have developed around body image will likely remain pressing ones.

CHAPTER 1

WHAT IS BODY IMAGE?

In one sense, understanding the concept of body image is easy. The *Merriam-Webster OnLine* dictionary defines body image as "a subjective picture of one's own physical appearance established both by self-observation and by noting the reactions of others."[1] This definition simply means that men and women are influenced in two ways when they think about body image. First, by what they think about their physical appearance when they look in the mirror or try on a new piece of clothing; and second, by what others—friends, families, and acquaintances—say about their physical appearance. The National Eating Disorders Association offers a more detailed definition of body image:

- How you see yourself when you look in the mirror or when you picture yourself in your mind.

- What you believe about your own appearance (including your memories, assumptions, and generalizations).

- How you feel about your body, including your height, shape, and weight.

- How you sense and control your body as you move. How you feel *in* your body, not just *about* your body.[2]

In another sense, these definitions provide only a bare outline for understanding body image. The concept of body image can be better comprehended with an understanding of its history— whether people have always held the same beliefs about body image or whether these beliefs have changed throughout history; whether, for instance, people today think about body image in the same way that people thought about body image in England or Tahiti during the 1800s. Body image, then, is influenced by many factors including customs, tradition, culture, and history.

An attempt to understand these different influences on the concept of body image is an attempt to understand the central role that body image plays in men's and women's lives. Researchers Thomas Pruzinsky and Thomas F. Cash explain:

> The vital role of body image means that it has the potential to dramatically influence our quality of life. From early childhood on, body image affects our emotions, thoughts, and behaviors in everyday life. Perhaps most poignantly, body image influences our relationships—those that are public as well as the most intimate.[3]

What Is Body Image?

Everyone has a body image, and it is normal to want to be attractive. Body image, however, is a much broader concept than attractiveness. Body image is a person's perception of his or her own physical appearance and what that person believes other people think of it. This image includes physical attractiveness, but it also includes clothing and general presentation (hair, makeup, shoes, etc.). When men and women look in the mirror and ask "Am I attractive?" and "Will my friends like my new outfit?" they are assessing body image. When men and women comment on the physical appearance of people they see in magazines, on billboards, and on television, they are also assessing body image.

An individual's concept of his or her own body image, however, does not always match his or her physical appearance. "Even though people say that 'the mirror doesn't lie,'" notes clinician Barbara Moe, "the mental picture we form about our bodies is often totally different from the actual appearances of our bodies."[4] It is common, for instance, for many individuals to believe that they weigh more than they do or that they are overweight when they are not. "Studies show that more than 60 percent of female high-school students believe they are overweight, when in fact less than 20 percent really are,"[5] writes social worker and author Diane Yancey. The difference between these two images can lead to inner conflict,

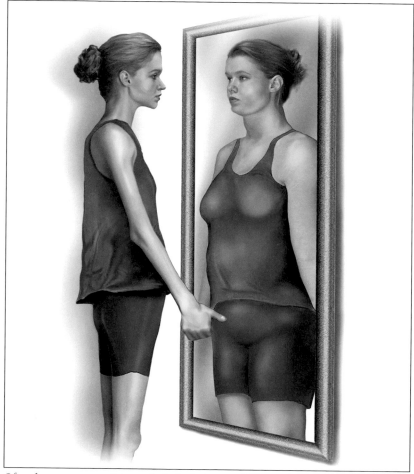

Often how a person pictures their body is very different from their actual appearance.

especially when an individual believes he or she is overweight, potentially influencing that person's overall self-assessment.

In many Western cultures, so much emphasis is placed on body image that it may seem synonymous with self-image. Self-image, however, is a broader concept that includes a person's physical, spiritual, and mental selves. Because physical appearance has become so important in contemporary culture, however, body image is frequently connected to self-esteem. "In industrialized cultures, body images, including perception of overall physical appearance, is probably the most important component of an adolescent's global self-esteem," observe psychologists Michael P. Levine and Linda Smolak. "The connection may be stronger during adolescence than in other age periods."[6] Concern over weight, height, and appearance may be normal, but it can also have a negative impact on adolescent body image if it does not match a person's idealized image.

Positive and Negative Body Image

Men and women develop both positive and negative body images. Generally, people with a positive body image are satisfied with their appearance and believe others also view them positively. The National Eating Disorders Association offers the following definition of a positive body image:

- A clear, true perception of your shape—you see the various parts of your body as they really are.

- You celebrate and appreciate your natural body shape and you understand that a person's physical appearance says very little about their character and value as a person.

- You feel proud and accepting of your unique body and refuse to spend an unreasonable amount of time worrying about food, weight, and calories.

- You feel comfortable and confident in your body.[7]

Dissatisfaction with one's physical appearance can lead to a negative body image. A common example would be worrying about gaining weight. Simply put, "it [negative body image] means that no matter how our body looks to others, we don't think it looks good enough," writes clinical psychologist Joni E. Johnston. "If a teenager or adult believes themselves to be overweight and perceive that the culture they live in considers an overweight person unattractive, then they may internalize a negative body image."[8] The National Eating Disorders Association defines negative body image in the following way:

- A distorted perception of your shape—you perceive parts of your body unlike they really are.

- You are convinced that only other people are attractive and that your body size or shape is a sign of personal failure.

- You feel ashamed, self-conscious, and anxious about your body.

- You feel uncomfortable and awkward in your body.[9]

Shifting Ideas About Body Image

When thinking about how an individual develops a personal concept of body image, turning to history can be helpful. Ideas about body image have changed frequently over time. Whether the issue is weight—who is considered thin and who is considered obese—or beauty—who is considered stunning and who is con-

Self-Criticism

When considering body image, it is easy for most men and women to worry about what other people think. Still, the worst criticism is often self-criticism. Emily Starr, writing in *No Body's Perfect*, indentifies her worst critic.

It is often said that seeing is believing; yet when it comes to one's own reflection, I've never found that statement to possess any truth. In fact, hearing is often believing. There was once this girl, and every day when she saw me she would sneer and say, "You're hideous." "You're fat." "Your complexion is horrible." "Your outfit looks stupid." She said these things over and over

again till I just buried my head in my hands and sobbed uncontrollably every time I saw my own reflection. She was right, I told myself. She was right about everything. The words were constantly echoing in my mind, ringing in my ears, screaming in my face. And that girl wasn't a bully at school or an enemy on the soccer field. She didn't have a crush on my boyfriend or any reason to hate me with so much passion. She was me. My tormentor was myself.

Kimberly Kirberger, *No Body's Perfect: Stories by Teens About Body Image, Self-Acceptance, and the Search for Identity.* New York: Scholastic, 2003, p. 75.

sidered average—standards have continued to shift throughout time and across cultures.

CULTURAL MESSAGES AND BODY IMAGE

"My sense[of] self-esteem too often depends on how I see my body, and my body image is increasingly affected (infected?) by a continuous, arbitrary onslaught of images and messages that dictate the rights and wrongs of physical appearance."—Chris Godsey, a journalist who blogs about body image issues.

Chris Godsey, "How Does It Feel?" Adios Barbie.com, September 2008. www.adiosbarbie.com/features/features_godsey.html.

Researchers have many theories about why weight and beauty standards fluctuate. One popular theory speculates that ideal weight revolves around wealth and poverty. In many poor cultures where food is scarce, a big body has often been considered healthy and attractive. With women, healthiness also seemed to symbolize the ability to have children within traditional cultures. If men and women were overweight in traditional cultures, it is because they were prosperous. Writing about prosperity in current China, Rachel Huxley and YangFeng Wu note,

"In Chinese culture, there is still a widespread belief that excess body fat represents health and prosperity. This may be a consequence of the famines and chronic malnutrition that caused millions of deaths in the past two centuries."[10] In wealthier countries like the United States today, where the majority of people can eat as much as they wish, body weight no longer represents prosperity. Thinness, sociologists have suggested, may now represent higher social status.

Historically, opinions about weight and beauty have often been more focused on women than men. Various arguments have attempted to explain why this is true. One argument states that because marriage was considered necessary for the upper- and middle-class women who seldom worked and frequently could not inherit property, social pressure focused on women's attractiveness.

Middle- and upper-class men, on the other hand, would have been more defined by a profession or wealth. In the contemporary world, however, many social observers believe this focus is changing.

Customs and Traditions

Many changes in how body image has been viewed are connected to cultural customs, such as the binding of feet in ancient China. Beginning in around 1000 A.D., the upper classes in China believed that the practice of foot binding enhanced women's beauty. "A pair of perfectly bound feet must meet seven qualifications—small, thin, pointed, arched, fragrant, soft, and straight—in order to become a piece of art, an object of erotic desire,"[11] writes author Wang Ping. Over time, the tradition of foot binding became fashionable. The process of binding a woman's foot, however, was long and painful, requiring the displacement of the natural bone structure and requiring special shoes. Women with bound feet had limited mobility and walked in small steps. Perhaps the

Foot Binding

The long history of foot binding in China only came to an end in the 1900s. The practice of foot binding altered the curvature of women's feet and was considered an attractive feature for women, especially among the upper classes. Wang Ping describes one girl's experience with foot binding—her own, recalled in third person in *Aching for Beauty: Footbinding in China.*

> At the age of nine she began to bind her feet on her own. She did not know the elaborate method of the traditional footbinding. . . . She invented her own method of binding, wrapping her feet tightly with layers of elastic bands to prevent her feet from growing longer and wider. Though she did not bend her toes under her soles or break her bones, it still hurt. Her bandaged feet were on fire day and night. Each step felt as though she were walking on broken glass barefooted. But she bore the pain silently, and with much pride. She was determined to keep her feet from growing.

Wang Ping, *Aching for Beauty: Footbinding in China.* New York: Anchor, 2000, p. ix.

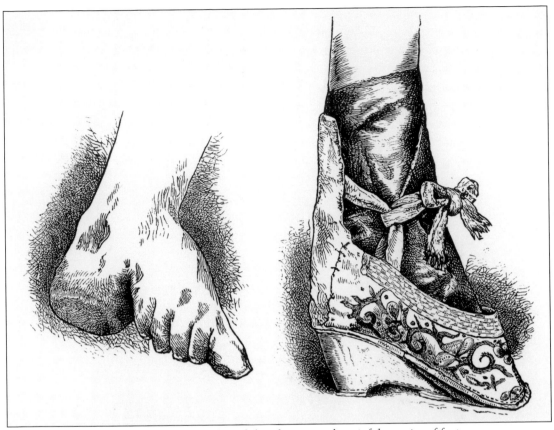

Around 1000 A.D. China believed that the extremely painful practice of foot binding enhanced a woman's beauty.

biggest irony of foot binding was that it was difficult to keep a bound foot clean because of folds in the skin, allowing for the growth of fungi and producing an odor. The practice of foot binding continued in China into the 1900s when more modern traditions began to consider foot binding old-fashioned and elitist.

In other eras, tradition and custom influenced the development of body image in different ways. In Europe during the 1600s, for instance, many people considered plumpness as pleasing. "Plumpness was considered fashionable and erotic until relatively recently,"[12] notes researcher Sarah Grogan. This perspective is exemplified in the art of Peter Paul Rubens, a Flemish painter in the 1600s. The women who appeared in his paintings, including

Bibliothèque Saint-Claude Library

Rubens's wife Helene, were variously described as fleshy, plump, and voluptuous. "The women Rubens celebrated in his art," writes author Shari Graydon, "boast dimpled thighs, ample arms, and ripples of fat around their bodies."[13] The women that Rubens painted for commissions, however, were frequently wealthy and may have weighed more than women of the lower classes during the same time period.

As in Europe, ideals about body image would change over time in the United States. Researcher Barbara A. Cohen writes that women in colonial America (before 1776) were bigger and more muscular and considered both attractive and healthy. She says:

> This was a period of time in the history of our country in which size and strength were important assets for a woman to possess, for her own survival as well as her desirability as a wife, mother and worker of the land. Her fertility was important because the more children she could produce, the more free labor or helpers the family would have to work the land.[14]

Fashionable Body Types

Ideas about beauty shifted near the end of the 1800s in the United States. While traditions would overlap the newer trends, the fashion industry and national magazines would increasingly influence body ideals. An early example of this influence is the craze in the United States for the Gibson girl between the 1890s and World War I (1917).

The Gibson girl, drawn for magazines by illustrator Charles Dana Gibson, would become the ideal for younger women. While she retained an hourglass figure and the full bosom of the ideal Victorian woman, her waist—held in by a corset—was slender. By exchanging frilly petticoats with the more practical blouse, the Gibson girl also revealed her figure more. Energetic and on the go, she represented youthful exuberance and the changing roles for women within American society.

The wide circulation of these periodicals also offered a new way for people to learn about trends in fashion. Whereas men and women would have been aware of primarily local ideals of beauty in traditional cultures, the appearance of the Gibson girl in new magazines in the late 1800s such as *Ladies Home Journal*, helped spread these ideals nationally. "The Gibson girl swept the nation," notes Bob Batchelor in *The 1900s*. "Her image could be found everywhere, from pinups on college campuses to the Alaskan Klondike."[15]

Then came the neatly dressed Gibson man. With his hair slicked back and parted in the middle, combined with a square

Opera singer Lillian Russell lost weight to achieve a more hourglass-type figure.

'ER'S WEEKLY.

Thomson's New Styles
Glove - Fitting Corset.

All Infringers of our Patents,
or of our Copyright
in Names,
Will be Prosecuted.

THE VENTILATING OR SUMMER CORSET.
Entirely NEW in Style and Perfect in Shape.
The **Curvilinear**, rich and elegant in finish.
Also, a lower cost "**Glove-Fitting**" than ever
before offered; which, with our former regular qual-
ities, make the assortment complete.
These justly celebrated PATENT GLOVE-FIT-
TING CORSETS are constantly gaining favor in the
United States as well as in foreign countries.
Always ask for **Thomson's** GENUINE GLOVE-
FITTING, every Corset being Stamped.
THOMSON, LANGDON, & CO.,
Sole Patentees,   **391 BROADWAY, N. Y.**

J. J. H. GREGORY'S
SEED CATALOGUE.
My Annual Illustrated Catalogue, containing a list
of many new and rare Vegetables, some of which are
not found in any other catalogue, and all the standard

Advertisement for a corset in 1871. Women wore tight corsets to make their waists appear smaller.

jaw and clean-shaven face, he was seen as the ideal companion for the Gibson girl. Like her, he represented a youthful idea that appealed to a younger generation. Both the Gibson girl and boy also emphasized new, more open attitudes toward body image in the United States.

These social changes that allowed more choice in the public display of bodies in the United States—especially women's bodies—would continue in the 1920s with the birth of the flapper. Flappers wore short, straight dresses called shifts that de-emphasized women's hips and breasts while emphasizing bare legs (from the knees down) and bare arms. Flappers refused to wear the traditional corset that had accentuated the curvature of the body, and they rolled their stockings down to their knees in order to make dancing easier. They also rebelled against tradition by bobbing or shortening their hair. The flapper look was modern, representing freedom of movement, the growing number of women in the workplace, and changing ideas about sexuality.

From Twiggy to Today

In the United States the ideal represented by the flapper would fade in the postwar 1940s into French designer Christian Dior's more opulent "New Look" of padded shoulders, pinched waists, and layers of petticoats. During the social upheaval of the 1960s, however, many of the trends started by the flapper would be revived. These trends included a return to shorter skirts and dresses and changes in social mores, including new ideas about women's independence and sexuality.

A number of social observers pinpoint obsession with thinness to the mid-1960s in Britain and the United States, a trend that was perhaps symbolized by the appearance of a model named Twiggy. In 1966, the sixteen-year-old single-named Twiggy became a supermodel in England and the following year debuted in the United States. "Twiggy was the forerunner of all waiflike, broomstick-thin models of today,"[16] write authors Dorothy Hoobler and Thomas Hoobler. She weighed 91 pounds (41.3kg), and with small hips and no noticeable breasts, she represented an androgynous or unisex style. Many fashion designers found the new, thinner style the ideal form of youth and beauty to display current lines of clothing in *Cosmopolitan* and other women's magazines.

Other trends in fashion during the 1960s would strengthen this new development of the thinner body style. Most prominent among these was the popularity of the bikini in the 1960s, a style of bathing suit that favored women with long legs and thin, Twiggy-like figures. "Fleshy curves that spilled out of the Band-Aid top and postage-stamp bottom looked gross," writes feminist Susan Brownmiller. "A less endowed figure looked more esthetically pleasing."[17]

BEAUTY IS NOT UNIVERSAL

"In many societies, good looks equals a good body. But again, even the societies that worship fine bodies do not agree on what constitutes a good body."—Elaine Hatfield, professor of psychology, and Susan Sprecher, professor of sociology.

Elaine Hatfield and Susan Sprecher, *Mirror, Mirror: The Importance of Looks in Everyday Life*. Albany, NY: New York Press, 1986.

Social observers have also noted that while the thin body style may be dominant, it always overlaps with other sometimes contradictory trends. In American culture during the 1990s, for instance, models like Pamela Anderson had a thin body and large breasts. Often models and actresses achieved a similar look with breast implant surgery. Other models like Britain's Sophie Dahl, however, became known for a more voluptuous or full-bodied look. Reporter Joanna Rahim referred to Dahl as a "voluptuous size 14 figure." She writes, "Normally, this would not be news. Most women in Britain are larger than a size 12. What is news, however, is that in an industry where being a size 10 is pushing it, Sophie is this year's [1997] hottest model."[18]

Even if one body style remains more popular or noticeable at a particular time period, other styles continue to emerge.

A number of social observers have suggested that a new body style based on physical fitness has become ascendant or at least a strong competitor for the thin body style in contemporary America. "Now it is muscle tone, skin tone, and 'being in shape,'" writes author Hillel Schwartz, "rather than an insistent call to the scales."[19] Since the 1980s Americans have seen the growth of the exercise industry, and today millions of men and women have joined gyms. This trend has also been supported by a greater awareness that better eating habits and regular exercise could lead to a healthier lifestyle. "In the '70s and '80s, we exercised and dieted excessively to achieve the Twiggy model image," wrote Gilda Marx in *American Fitness*. "Now we know ultra-thinness is not healthy."[20]

How Do Biology and Culture Affect Body Image

Perhaps the first factor that affects body image is one that a person has relatively little control over: biology. Everyone is born with the genes of their parents, and these genes help determine body shape. Because of this, the actual control a person has over his or her physical appearance can be understood by looking at the influence of genetics and biology on physical development.

But understanding the influence of biology is just the beginning of comprehending the development of body image. Within any given culture, a wide range of factors can influence how men and women understand body image. One of the earliest influences may stem from one's immediate home and the lessons children learn from parents, siblings, and guardians. These influences can also include friends at school and extended-family members such as grandparents. Boys and girls will frequently learn their first lessons about body image from watching the behavior of parents and guardians. They may also learn that family and friends have expectations in relation to body image issues and may be willing to use their influence to shape how others feel about these issues.

Another influence on body image revolves around expectations of physical shape and attractiveness relating to age. Body image is seldom a stable concept, and ideas about body image may change as one grows older. As one ages from a child to an adult or from middle age to senior status, the physical body continues to evolve. Adolescents, for instance, frequently experience growth spurts and body development during teenage years; older adults may develop wrinkles or lose hair. These physical changes

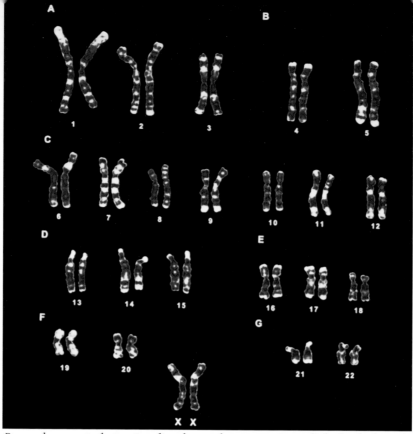

Research suggests that eating disorders such as anorexia are linked to biological factors, including chromosomes.

may create instability as individuals attempt to adjust to alterations in personal appearance.

Biological Influences

While customs, fashion, and culture will influence ideas about body images, these influences also must work within other boundaries that affect both body style and the development of body image. For instance, a man or a woman may find it difficult or even impossible to adhere to a current style because of the shape of his or her body. Many factors that contribute to body shape and the development of body image are biological and inherited at birth from parents.

Biology is a constant influence on body type. Every person's body type and personal qualities—hair and eye color, shape, and height—are influenced by the genetics and biology of his or her parents. "The genes passed down from your ancestors through your biological parents are yours forever, good and bad,"[21] note authors of *The Complete Idiot's Guide to Healthy Weight Loss* Lucy Beale and Sandy G. Couvillon. Parents and distant relatives provide a distinct genetic code and a singular biology that shape and limit the possibilities of one's physical form.

Researchers today also speculate that one's gene pool may impact a number of body image issues. For instance, a person may be born with a high metabolism (the rate at which the body processes calories) that prevents him or her from gaining weight quickly. Another person may be born with a malfunctioning thyroid gland that aids weight gain. "Each person has a unique profile of genes, biology and lifestyle,"[22] notes journalist Emma Ross. These genes will help determine the shape of an individual's body, height, and eye color.

Besides impacting how bodies grow, Smolak has noted that the strongest connection between biology and body image issues may be indirect. If biology impacts eating patterns, children may be born with a tendency to overeat and become obese. "The feeling of hunger is intense and, if not as potent as the drive to breathe, is probably no less powerful than the drive to drink when one is thirsty," notes researcher Jeffrey M. Friedman.[23] In relation to body image, individual temperament, or personality, and biology are also connected. Temperament relates to qualities like emotion and mood or the fact that some children seem basically content while others are fussy. Whereas theorists had previously argued that the social influence of friends, families, and peers were more important to a child's development than biological influences like temperament, a number of researchers are now rethinking these conclusions.

Feedback from Family, Siblings, and Friends

After biology, one of the earliest influences relating to the formation of body image is a child's family or home environment. Important influences include comments by a parental figure on a child's appearance, modeling (how the parent relates to his or her own body image), and the feedback the child receives from parents and guardians. Johnston explains, "As individuals . . . we each have a unique beauty history. Some of our families were

Positive comments by parents about their child's weight can lead to a more positive body image.

more concerned about looks than others. Growing up, we each received different feedback about our looks from friends and family members."[24]

Peers, including friends and classmates, can also play an important role in the development of body image. As with parents, peer feedback and teasing can help shape attitudes and influence body image ideals.

Direct Comments

One important aspect of the parent-child communication in relation to body image is referred to by psychologists as "direct comments." This means that a parent has offered feedback to the child about his or her weight, hair, or general appearance. "Parents can influence body image development by selecting and commenting on children's clothing and appearance, or by requiring the child to look certain ways and to eat or avoid certain foods,"[25] writes Smolak. Some research has suggested that positive comments by parents on a child's weight or appearance can lead to a more positive body image.

Research has also found, however, that parents or guardians frequently offer negative comments regarding weight, suggesting, for example, that a child should eat less or exercise more in an effort to slim down. These comments may be connected to negative feelings in relation to a child's body image. "Things we hear growing up have an impact on us as adults," writes Johnston. "Not only do they shape the way we view ourselves, they directly affect our adult behavior."[26]

Researchers have also wondered whether these direct comments affect boys and girls equally. Some theorists have suggested that women receive more pressure to conform to what is considered an attractive body style within a given culture and because of this, parents may focus their body image comments more directly on girls than boys. A number of studies, however, have shown that parents are equally critical of boys and girls in regard to weight. Girls, however, may be more affected by this criticism than boys, perhaps accounted for by other influences outside of the home. "Girls are exposed to more direct messages about the importance of looks and, not surprisingly," notes Johnston, "these messages often result in a focus on appearance as we grow up."[27]

POWERFUL INFLUENCES

"Since parents are such powerful influences, teens often 'buy into' the messages of their parents even when they are not really comfortable with such messages. . . . Many teens have trouble reconciling the messages they receive from their parents with those they receive from society."—Diane Yancey, social worker and author.

Diane Yancey, *Eating Disorders*. Brookfield, CT: Twenty-First Century, 1999, p. 69.

The influence of direct comments can also take place between friends and schoolmates. Direct comments about one or the other's appearance are called feedback. This feedback, however, may be delivered in a variety of ways. For instance, a person might comment positively on what his or her friend is wearing ("Cool shoes!" or "I really like that dress!") or negatively ("Does your Mom make your clothes?" or "Did you buy that at the thrift shop?"). Positive and negative feedback by peers, like direct comments by adults, offers information that may be influential in the development of body image.

Parents and Body Image

In Elaine Landau's *The Beauty Trap*, Krista recalls how her mother's obsession with weight affected her own body image.

My mother is really nuts when it comes to weight and appearance. She thinks there's nothing more important for a girl than looking good. My sister agrees with her, and the two of them have been on a lifelong diet. I love them both, but it's hard to be around Leah and Mom. I'm not fat, but I'm not a size 4 either, and they consider a girl who's size 12 unsightly.

Maybe I'd like to be thinner, but whenever I've taken off weight I've always put it back on within months. Before the divorce my father used to tell my mother to leave me alone but she'd tell him not to shield me from the truth. I guess to her the truth was that I was fat and not making the most of my looks.

Elaine Landau, *The Beauty Trap*. New York: New Discovery, 1994, pp. 35–36.

Modeling, Peer Pressure, Teasing

Whereas the influence of direct comments by parents and friends may appear fairly straightforward, other influences on the development of body image such as modeling are more difficult to measure. In modeling, a child learns by watching what a parent does or by listening to what a parent says about his or her own body image. By observing a parent's behavior, for instance, a child may develop the same habits. If a parent comments frequently on his or her own weight, a child may learn that body weight is something that should be monitored closely. Modeling is also complicated by the fact that a parent may send contradictory messages. For example, a father may say one thing—"Your personality is more important than your looks"—but then offer critical comments about his own weight.

Perhaps the most potentially harmful feedback to one's concept of body image is teasing, whether from family or peers. "Teasing, in particular," write scientists Stacey Tantleff-Dunn and Jessica L. Gokee, "is an experience common to most children and foreign to few adults." Teasing has a great impact on adolescents, who may internalize teasing as self-criticism. "Researchers have found that being teased is one of the most commonly reported precipitants of body dissatisfaction." [28]

Another issue that impacts the development of body image in both adults and children is peer pressure. Studies have shown peer pressure among teenagers to be influential with behavior such as drinking alcohol, smoking cigarettes, and taking drugs. Many researchers believe that peer pressure may also influence the willingness of teenagers to conform to popular body image types. While peer pressure may be generally thought of as a problem for teenagers, other studies have shown adult peer pressure is similarly influential with behavior such as smoking. At work as with school, peer pressure may play a role on the willingness of adults to conform to popular body image types.

Gender and Body Image

When focusing on body image and how body image develops, many researchers have studied whether these issues impact boys and girls differently. In the past, feminists and other social critics commonly argued that girls and women are taught by culture to focus on body image more intensely than boys and men. *Empowered Parents*, a Web site dedicated to body image issues, notes,

"A U.S. Dept. of Health and Human Services task force reports that 80% of girls in grades 3–6 have bad feelings about their bodies, an issue diverting attention from schoolwork and friendships." In more recent times, however, sociologists have begun to suggest that the culture has an equal impact

An overweight boy hides from boys who are teasing him. Criticism from peers can have a deep impact on a child.

on boys and men. "Preteen boys as well," notes the *Empowered Parents* Web site, "inspired by the world of sports and television, fret about the inadequacy of their builds, believing that the strength in their muscles or the girth in their chests is more important than intelligence, compassion or emotional well-being."[29]

Girls

A number of studies in the United States have focused on the body image concerns of girls and women. The U.S. Department

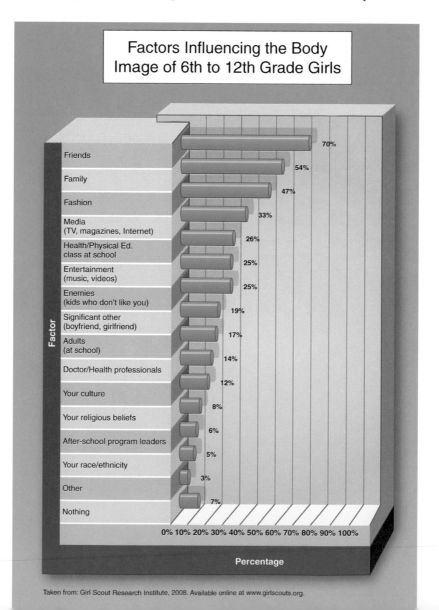

Factors Influencing the Body Image of 6th to 12th Grade Girls

Factor	Percentage
Friends	70%
Family	54%
Fashion	47%
Media (TV, magazines, Internet)	33%
Health/Physical Ed. class at school	26%
Entertainment (music, videos)	25%
Enemies (kids who don't like you)	25%
Significant other (boyfriend, girlfriend)	19%
Adults (at school)	17%
Doctor/Health professionals	14%
Your culture	12%
Your religious beliefs	8%
After-school program leaders	6%
Your race/ethnicity	5%
Other	3%
Nothing	7%

0% 10% 20% 30% 40% 50% 60% 70% 80% 90% 100%

Percentage

Taken from: Girl Scout Research Institute, 2008. Available online at www.girlscouts.org.

of Health and Human Services notes: "Is your body image positive or negative? If your answer is negative, you are not alone. Women in the U.S. are under pressure to measure up to a certain social and cultural ideal of beauty, which can lead to poor body image."[30]

One persistent concern involves weight, with girls and women wishing to be thinner than they are. While studies have revealed contradictory results, some estimate that half of the girls between six and eight years old wish that they were thinner. Some studies suggest that body dissatisfaction may begin at an even earlier age. "Negative attitudes toward overweight emerge very early," note researchers Ruth H. Striegel-Moore and Debra L. Franko.

Studies have shown that females—throughout their lifetime—are more concerned with body image than men.

"Indeed, stigmatization of overweight children is already present in 3-year-olds."[31]

While no cause can be isolated, research suggests that girls and women internalize a thin ideal from the culture in which they live from a variety of sources including family, friends, the media, and advertising. Once that thin ideal has been internalized, girls and women will compare their weight with that of a person who fits the ideal image. If they believe they have fallen short of that ideal, they may develop a negative body image and possibly eating disorders in an attempt to reach the desired weight. These concerns may also lead to psychological problems that extend beyond body image issues, including low self-esteem and depression. "Females are much more likely than males to experience body image concerns, regardless of age,"[32] note Striegel-Moore and Franko.

Boys

While the idea is generally accepted that girls and women experience more body image concerns than boys and men, research suggests that this phenomenon may be changing. While fewer studies have been conducted with boys, the available research suggests that body image concerns begin in preadolescence for boys. "There are many indications that body dissatisfaction in boys and men is becoming an increasingly common source of much suffering,"[33] note Patricia Westmoreland Corson and Arnold E. Andersen. Researchers also note that advertising has focused more heavily on boys and men in recent years. The percentage of men with such eating disorders has also continued to climb in recent years, though statistics have not always supported this claim. Also suggested, however, is that "shame and fear of public humiliation drove men with body image dissatisfaction and eating disorders 'underground.'"[34]

Despite similarities to the body issue concerns expressed by girls and women, however, boys and men have focused on body issues in dissimilar ways. While boys and men are frequently concerned with thinness, they also frequently focus on muscle mass. Studies have shown that a woman is likely to overestimate her weight, while a man may underestimate his. Whereas many women focus on becoming thinner, many men focus on adding muscle mass to achieve a specific body shape.

Children and Adolescents

Children seem to be affected by body image stereotypes from an early age, partly as a result of parental influence. One study at Florida State University focused on three-year-olds and noted that parents of these children had already begun to express concern with weight issues. Other researchers have focused on the age that children begin to have a concept of body image. Research suggests that four- and five-year-olds have already developed ideas on what it means to be fat, including prejudices against being overweight. Through interaction with adults and peers and perhaps through advertising, children develop images of people who are considered overweight. Many researchers believe that children internalize these images of obese persons and judge their own weight against these images. Smolak has noted that children as young as six years old "express body dissatisfaction and weight concerns."[35]

While children have clearly formulated an idea of body image before adolescence, researchers believe that these issues become more important to boys and girls as they reach their teenage years. The reason primarily revolves around the physical and hormonal changes experienced during puberty along with the beginning of romantic attachments. At this point in their lives, adolescents experience many physical changes and become more aware of how others may see them. At school, for instance, boys and girls may become more aware of weight and appearance and may expend more time on developing social relationships than on school studies. These issues may place more pressure on body image concerns.

Adults

Although physical changes may be less sudden after adolescence, adults continue to experience physical changes and with those changes, new body image concerns. Some studies suggest that men and women face cultural prejudice as they grow older; as people develop wrinkles, gray hair, lose muscle mass, develop fragile bones, and lose height, their appearance may clash with the culture's ideals of youth and beauty. Many adults also frequently begin to gain weight in their forties, partly because the body's metabolism begins to slow down. As a result, women may believe that wrinkles and a heavier body detract from the thin, youthful ideal; men may believe that loss of muscle mass or the loss of hair may likewise detract from a muscular, youthful appearance. Within a culture that idealizes youth and youthful bodies, some men and women may consider multiple methods to alter body image, from exercise and healthy eating to cosmetic surgery.

As adults grow older, gender issues may continue to separate the sexes in regard to body image ideals. "Signs of aging in men may be seen to make them look more 'distinguished,'" notes Grogan,

As men age, they may believe that loss of muscle mass or hair may detract from their appearance.

"whereas in women (who are often judged in terms of physical attractiveness rather than in terms of abilities or experience) signs of aging may be seen negatively both by others and by themselves."[36] This difference seems to be based on the idea that men are perceived as gaining career-related experience and competency along with a secure economic status as they grow older. In some studies, however, women have been shown to depend less on appearance for self-esteem after sixty, perhaps because physical appearance has become less important.

Body Image and Age

While men and women may approach body image issues in a variety of ways, both will frequently need to make adjustments in their personal concept of body image as they age. At different ages, men and women often become concerned with different body image issues. This is partly because the body continues to change as they grow older. While it is common knowledge that boys and girls experience rapid physical change during adolescence, the human body continues to change in a variety of ways in adulthood. As women and men reach middle age, for instance, they develop wrinkles. These changes impact how they think about body image issues.

Even as people age, however, many of the concerns surrounding body image remain the same over the course of their life spans. One example, especially with women, is a concern with weight. While this concern may be expressed in different ways at different ages, it nonetheless remains a concern. Another example would be concern with general attractiveness. Most men

Aging and Body Image

In *Beautiful Again: Restoring Your Image and Enhancing Body Changes*, Jan Willis addresses a reality that each person faces as he or she grows older: his or her appearance will change.

The image we see in the mirror—our reflective image—affects the way we act, the way we feel about ourselves, and the way we relate to others. Conversely, that same image often affects the way other people relate to us. Since appearance and self-esteem usually go hand in hand, what happens to our self-esteem when negative changes occur in our appearance?

Much of what we read and see relates to preserving youth. We live in a youth-oriented society, and most people feel that aging lowers their self-esteem. Aging gracefully and accepting others for what they are (and not for what they appear to be) seem to be endangered qualities; however, people are living longer and finding ways to prolong youth, at least in their mental outlook and appearance. . . .

As long as a person is reasonably healthy and active, it is assumed that he or she will be concerned about personal looks.

Jan Willis, *Beautiful Again: Restoring Your Image & Enhancing Body Changes*. Santa Fe, NM: Health Press, 1994, p. 17.

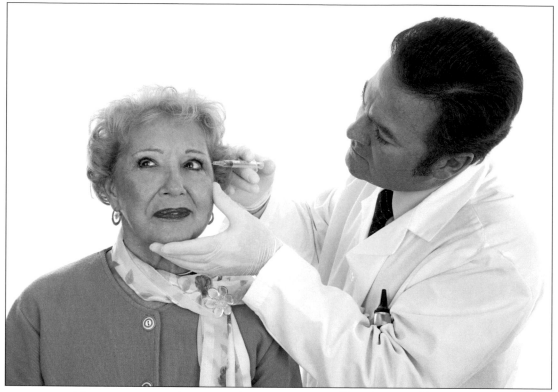

Many women opt to have cosmetic surgery to try and lose their wrinkles and appear more youthful.

and women, from childhood to senior status, wish to be considered attractive. As with weight, however, how these concerns are expressed will vary at different ages.

When considering how ideas about aging and body image change over a person's life span, it is also import to understand the limitations of many studies relating to body image on men and women over twenty-five. Commonly, researchers have used college students between eighteen and twenty-five for many studies. Still, the body of information available on adults over twenty-five continues to grow.

CHAPTER 3

Do Mass Media Distort Ideas of Body Image?

Many factors impact body image, from biology to the influence of family and friends and from gender to the changes that take place during the aging process. These factors, however, work within a broader, everyday cultural environment. While people may be influenced about body image issues at home and school, they also learn about body image through mass media. The media are essentially modern phenomenona that date back to the mid-1800s and represent companies that can reach mass audiences through radio, CDs, magazines, newspapers, television, movies, books, video games, and the Internet. By offering millions of images of other men and women every day, the media have the potential to serve as a powerful influence on contemporary life.

Because the images made available by the media are so pervasive, it is helpful to have a better understanding of how the media may impact the daily lives of men and women. A number of social observers believe that people may learn body image lessons—about weight, hair color, clothing style, height, and facial structure—every time they watch a sitcom, music video, or play a computer game.

Whether boys and girls play with Barbie dolls or GI Joes, watch videos of popular music artists, or look at photographs of models in fashion magazines, they are bombarded with body images. Many social critics believe these images are idealized and are a primary influence on people's beliefs about body images.

Other social critics have suggested that while the media may influence ideas about body image, they are hardly the only influence. These critics suggest that blaming the media is only an easy scapegoat for broader social problems. "Although it is tempting to blame today's media for perpetuating and glorifying unrealistic standards of physical beauty," write researchers Jennifer L. Derenne and Eugene V. Bersin, "the truth is far more complicated."[37]

THE MEDIA AFFECT BODY IMAGE

"Even on the remote island of Fiji, the arrival of television—and Western cultural values along with it—generated a sharp increase in eating disorders among adolescent girls."—Joan Jacobs Brumberg, anorexia nervosa historian.

Joan Jacobs Brumberg, *Fasting Girls: The History of Anorexia Nervosa,* rev. ed. New York: Vintage, 2000, p. xv.

Research in the United States and Europe is inconclusive on the media's effect on individuals. Even while studies have shown them to be influential, the media seem to impact individuals differently, and no study proves conclusively how long any particular influence will remain active. While many researchers and social critics are convinced that the media do affect how men and women think about body image, they also acknowledge that further studies are needed to fully comprehend the extent of their influence.

The Consumption of Media

Social critics have noted that the media have become so much a part of contemporary life that many people have difficulty recognizing their influence on issues like body image. Television, the movies, and the Internet, are simply woven into the fabric of everyday life, they argue. Because of this, the consumption of images has become integral to life in many developed countries like the United States and Canada.

Teenagers and adults are bombarded everyday with body images from mass media. The images appear in television programs and commercials, fashion magazines and newspaper articles, computer games and Internet videos, and on roadside billboards and stadium marquees. "The media surrounds us," observe authors David Croteau and William Hoynes. "Our everyday lives are saturated by radio, television, newspapers, books, the Internet, movies, recorded music, magazines, and more."[38]

The bombardment of body images is aided by contemporary society's steady diet of television, videos, magazines, and computer and video games. In a study issued by the *American Academy of Pediatrics* in 2005, a group sample of ten thousand boys and girls between the ages of twelve and eighteen was used to study media exposure. Boys watched an average of 12.3 hours of television per week while girls watched an average of 9.5 hours per week. The study also noted that nearly 77 percent of the girls surveyed frequently read fashion magazines while 28.6 percent of the boys read sports magazines. A 2005 study by Jupiter Research found that consumers were spending the same amount of time online as they did watching television, an average of fourteen

A Harris study found that teens spend an average of thirteen to fourteen hours a week playing video games. They can be influenced by the types of bodies they see in the games.

hours per week. A survey by Harris Interactive found that teens spend an average of thirteen to fourteen hours per week playing video games.

A study by the Council for Research Excellence reported similar findings for adults at the beginning of 2009. In conclusion, the study found that adults were spending an average of 8.5 hours per day exposed to TV, cell phones, and GPS devices. This consumption of screen time was also consistent across the expanse of most age groups, with the exception of those between forty-five and fifty-four, who spent 9.5 hours in front of a screen each day. Many considered these findings surprising because it was assumed that boys and girls who were under eighteen spent more time interacting with media than adults. These studies suggest that many teens and adults spend forty hours per week or more watching television, surfing the Internet, reading magazines, and playing computer and video games. As a result, teenagers and adults are exposed to thousands of media-created body images on a daily basis.

The Impact of the Media

While it is easy for social critics and researchers to agree that children and adults are consuming more media relating to body image than ever before, it is more difficult for observers to understand what increased consumption means for individuals. Many feminists, for instance, assert that the media is the leading cause of negative body image and low self-esteem, especially for women. Other social critics see

Fashion magazines can promote an unrealistic view of how a woman should look—incredibly thin with perfect skin. Teenagers often feel they can't compare to these women, which leads to a negative body image.

Barbie

The original Barbie that launched in 1959.

Barbie was launched by Mattel in 1959 and remains one of the world's most popular dolls. During its first year in production, 350,000 Barbie dolls were sold. Barbie's hourglass figure and thinness, however, have long led critics to ask: Is it possible for a real woman to look like Barbie? Author Shari Graydon observes:

> If Barbie . . . were a full-sized human being, her measurements would be 39-21-33; she'd have to have all of her clothes custom made.

> One academic expert figured out that a woman's chances of having a figure like Barbie's were less than one in 100,000.

Shari Graydon, *In Your Face: The Culture of Beauty and You.* New York: Annick, 2004, pp. 123-24.

the media as an easy scapegoat for broader social problems. Still other critics note that while the media may present idealized body images, they are nonetheless creating products that people choose to watch and read.

The multiple studies on the impact of media on adults, teens, and children in developed nations have also produced contradictory results. Even when studies find evidence for the influence of the media in the development of body image, it remains unclear how to weigh their influence compared to the influence of biology and culture. Another factor to consider is whether men and women are more vulnerable to the influence at different ages. For instance, many argue that teenagers are highly motivated to seek approval from their peers, and therefore, ideals of attractive body image on television may be more influential during one's teen years. Despite the lack of clear results, critics and defenders of the media's use of body image have continued to make strong arguments for their position.

A Distorted View of Society

Many feminists and media observers have opined that a central problem with the daily bombardment of body images is that the media often fail to represent all body types equally. Kate Fox, writing for the Social Issues Research Centre, notes the perceived influence of the media:

- Thanks to the media, we have become accustomed to extremely rigid and uniform standards of beauty.

- TV, billboards, magazines etc. mean that we see "beautiful people" all the time, more often than members of our own family, making exceptional good looks seem real, normal and attainable.

- Standards of beauty have in fact become harder and harder to attain, particularly for women. The current media ideal of thinness for women is achievable by less than 5% of the female population.[39]

As a result, the reality of everyday life—at home, work, and school—can seem distorted when compared to the media's version of reality. When watching a favorite television show or playing a favorite video game, for instance, one may notice that certain body types appear more often than others. Female models in fashion magazines may be predominantly white, tall, and thin; men, predominantly muscular with flat stomachs. "These images convey assumptions about what is desirable in our physical selves while dispensing with reality,"[40] notes science writer Brandon Keim. Because of makeup and plastic surgery, actors and models may appear to never age or gain weight. The media, these critics maintain, idealize body types in order to sell products or increase ratings.

THE MEDIA IS ONLY ONE OF MANY INFLUENCES

"The media is a formidable force, and one that is not going to change easily. However, it is not the only culprit; parental behaviors and family values play an important role in shaping children's development."

Jennifer L. Derenne and Eugene V. Bersin, "Body Image, Media, and Eating Disorders," *Academic Psychiatry*, June 2006. http://ap.psychiatryonline.org/cgi/content/full/30/3/257.

These critics also believe that continuous exposure to ideal body types in the media may lead men and women to internalize these images. "As a whole, the research supports a link between media exposure and body image,"[41] notes Marika Tiggemann. By looking at thin models in fashion magazines, for instance, women may internalize the idea of thinness; likewise, by looking at muscular men in fitness magazines, men may internalize the muscular ideal. By internalizing these images, men and women may adopt the body image standards of the people they see on television and in fashion magazines. "Appearance pressures in our society," writes Johnston, "can easily turn into chronic dissatisfaction with our appearance and a never-ending pursuit of self-improvement."[42]

Obtaining the slimness or muscular build of a fashion or fitness model, however, may not be realistic or even healthy for

GI Joe

GI Joe, short for Government Issue Joe, was issued by Hasbro in February 1964. Noting the popularity of Barbie, the company launched an 11.5-inch GI Joe as "America's Movable Fighting Man." While GI Joe received less criticism than Barbie over the years, social critics did notice significant changes in his body image over time: He became increasingly muscular. The Milwaukee School of Engineering notes: "GI Joe is to boys what Barbie is to girls. . . . Over the past 20 years, these GI Joe toys have grown more muscular and currently have sharper muscle definition. The GI Joe Extreme action figure, if extrapolated to a height of 5'10", would have larger biceps than any bodybuilder in history."

Milwaukee School of Engineering, "Body Image Dissatisfaction: A Growing Concern Among Men," September 2008. www.msoe.edu/life_at_msoe/current_student_resources/student_resources/counseling_services/newsletters_for_mental_health/body_image_dissatisfaction.shtml.

many people, health specialists emphasize. Achieving the perfect look, for instance, may be both time consuming and hard work. "Every model must spend hours each day on personal care," writes journalist Ian Halperin. "Cosmetics, skin care, hair care, body care, and fragrances are a daily routine."[43] Many models and actors enhance their appearance with cosmetic surgery and liposuction (the removal of fat by cosmetic surgery). Photographs of models in magazines are further refined by airbrushing and digital manipulation. Many actors and models have personal trainers and are able to dedicate several hours each day to working out. When men and women compare themselves to media figures and attempt to copy difficult or impossible standards, this can lead to a negative body image and low self-esteem.

Easy Scapegoats

Other social observers have been quick to point out that the media have been easy scapegoats for broader societal problems. A number of sociologists have opined that the ideas relating to body image in the media are simply a reflection of values within the larger culture. That would mean thin models in magazines and muscular men on television are ideals that society has already embraced, and the media simply reinforces these ideas. From this point of view, men and women idolize actors and models because they represent body image types that are considered attractive in a given culture. Because the media presentation of body images simply reflects the larger culture, they argue, it would be a mistake to blame the media as an influence in the formation of unrealistic body images.

These critics have also pointed out that not all media are operated by corporate forces seeking profit through idealized body images. Online social networking sites such as Facebook and MySpace connect millions of people and allow them to share media on the Internet. If images of thin models are posted on these networks, they are posted by people who choose to participate within these forums. The media, these observers maintain, are simply easier to blame rather than placing the responsibility on parents or society. While the media may play a role in the development of body image, they argue, they are only one of many items that influence body image issues.

This theory emphasizes the idea that men and women choose to participate in media of their own free will. Media companies, they argue, cannot force the public to view its programs or buy its products. The public simply enjoys watching television programs and movies that include actors who have body styles that are considered attractive. Blog writer Roxy Lee notes, "There is something inspirational about watching beautiful people."[44]

Another criticism of those who blame the media for creating negative body image ideals is that these theorists assume that men and women believe everything that a media source tells them. This seems to remove the possibility that the individual will weigh and perhaps reject information offered by media outlets. These critics also argue that boys and girls do not always interpret the body images presented by the media in the same way. For instance, feminists have argued that Barbie dolls have little resemblance to the average-shaped woman and that GI Joes have little resemblance to the average-shaped man. Many children, these critics argue, seem to recognize that Barbie and GI Joe are play toys, not representative models of humans.

Outspoken Critics and Media Change

Because the use of body image in the media is pervasive and because many critics believe that these images may be internalized by both men and women, a great deal of social criticism has been aimed at the media. Consumer groups have claimed that media images are now influencing boys and girls at younger ages; feminists have argued that models and movie stars are becoming increasingly thinner. Johnston argues that contemporary society has become so fixated on body image that it has developed appearance obsession."We who are appearance obsessed have certain patterns of thinking, feeling and behaving in relation to our appearance, and almost all of these result in an ongoing sense of failure and inadequacy."[45]

A number of actors have been outspoken critics on the media's portrayal of body images. Actors like America Ferrera and Kate Winslet have made a public issue out of the media's focus on thin women. "We're not all a size 2 and we're not all a size 0, and you know what? That's OK, because some of us like to eat!"[46] says Ferrera, best known for her role as Betty on the television show *Ugly Betty*. Winslet, one of the stars of *Titanic*, has also been vocal about weight issues. "I'm certainly not a sex symbol who doesn't eat," Winslet protested in 2003 when *GQ* magazine manipulated her cover photograph. "The retouching is excessive. I don't look like that and I don't have a desire to look like that. I haven't suddenly lost 30 pounds."[47]

As a result of criticism from actors and health officials, and because of general social concern for healthier body images, the media have changed their approach to body image in a number of instances. A number of fashion magazines that feature plus-sized models have been launched in recent years, including *Plus*, *Venus Divas*, and *World of Curves*; television programs like *America's Next Top Model* have also featured plus size models. In 2004 Dove launched a "Campaign for Real Beauty," a worldwide promotional effort that relied on women who were not professional models. The campaign launched a "Self-Esteem Fund" designed to "free the next generation from self-limiting stereotypes."[48]

Actress Kate Winslet has been vocal in the media about her weight and criticized a magazine for retouching photos of her to make her look thinner.

Conflicted Media Messages

While critics have noted that many of these changes in representing body image may be motivated by an attempt to sell products to new consumers, they have nonetheless greeted many of these changes as positive. Overall, these changes have allowed the media to display a wider variety of body styles.

Even with these changes, however, media messages about body image remain conflicted. One common complaint is that fashion and fitness magazines publish articles deemphasizing weight issues or exploring the dangers of steroid use while still featuring photo spreads of ultrathin models and overly muscular men. Even in magazines featuring plus size models, advertisements may send out inconsistent messages. "On one hand the magazine celebrates beauty and fashion at every size," notes an anonymous commenter on the social technology and media Web site *Viewpoints*, "but the other hand is indicating that we cannot possibly be happy to be plus size and that we must be on Weight Watchers."[49]

This conflicting message and others like it underline one last problem with understanding the media's influence on body image issues: The media seldom deliver a uniform body image message. Because of this non-uniform message and the variety of body images presented, some media observers have suggested that people have vastly different experiences with the media. As with most body image issues, more research will be needed to make definite claims about how people experience media and how the influence of media affects men's and women's concepts of body image.

DOES ADVERTISING DISTORT BODY IMAGE?

The combination of advertising and body image ideals is prevalent in developed countries like the United States. Unlike the media in general, advertising is directly concerned with selling products. "You could say that advertising is basically anything someone does to grab your attention," writes Graydon, "and hold onto it long enough to tell you how cool, fast, cheap, tasty, fun, rockin' or rad whatever they're selling is."[50] One way that advertisers get consumers' attention is by displaying body images.

Advertisements appear in all forms of media, such as a commercial on television, but can also be displayed in any physical

People are bombarded with advertisements everywhere—in magazines, on television, and on billboards while driving.

space (on the side of a city bus, for instance). This helps advertisers reach consumers in the home (television, radio, and the Internet) and in public spaces (billboards). Advertisements appear on traditional and electronic billboards, on Web pages, and even in the halls of many schools.

Advertisements featuring the body images of men and women are so much a part of contemporary culture, in fact, that many consumers are unaware of just how many they view on a daily basis. A recent study by the market research group Yankelovich estimated that people who live in an urban environment may see as many as five thousand advertisements per day. Yankelovich also estimated that this was approximately three thousand more advertisements than would have seen in an urban environment thirty years ago.

ADVERTISEMENTS PROMOTE AN UNREALISTIC GOAL

"There is growing belief that advertisers purposely create these unrealistic images of people in an effort to make people dislike themselves and their bodies. As long as people believe that they do not have the perfect body, they will be willing to spend money on products in an attempt to meet this goal."

"The Influence of Advertising on Body Image," February 2, 2009. Saskatchewan Schools, www.saskschools.ca/. Saskatchewan Schools is a network of learning centers in Canada.

As with the media, many of these advertisements use body image to help sell products. This was a combination—advertising and body image—that bothered many public censors, even before researchers began studying its possible effect on men's and women's personal body images. Many of the criticisms of media—both positive and negative—could be applied to advertising. Both advertising and the media have been accused by feminists and health experts of distorting body image. Writer Allen Teal underlines these common criticisms: "From hairstyles to body shape to shoes on our feet, advertising tries to persuade us that to look our best, we must have the body that society now considers ideal."[51]

Likewise, the public has often criticized the use of sex or sexuality in advertising, complaining that these images objectify male and female bodies and sexualize adolescent bodies. Furthermore, since advertisers frequently use thin female and muscular male models, these advertisements set up unrealistic goals and help create body image dissatisfaction. Numerous research studies focusing on body image and advertising, however, have produced inconclusive results.

The Use of Body Image in American Advertising

For a number of commentators, the use of body image in advertising has historically rested on two ideas. One, to offer images of whatever body type was considered ideal in any era, and two, to push the boundaries on what was allowable by public censors. These critics argue that advertisers have always been willing to distort or idealize body image to sell products. The history of the use of body image within American advertising, then, reveals the distortion of body image as a continuous and evolving phenomenon.

While multiple forms of advertising existed early in American history, few focused on displays of bodies. Socially, many Americans during the 1600s and 1700s may have believed that displaying bodies to sell products was immoral, according to religious beliefs of Puritans and others. With the advent of the industrial revolution during the 1800s, sociologists have noted, these community standards began to change as Americans began to relocate to cities. Advertising would take on a new urgency during this time as companies attempted to convince the public to buy items like clothing that people had formerly made at home. One of the ways that manufacturers would turn Americans into consumers during the 1800s was to use body image to sell new products.

By the 1880s magazines, photography, and advertising agencies were changing the face of American advertising. Many advertisers decided that associating an attractive person with a product would help to sell it. A Duke cigarette ad from 1888 features a schoolteacher

Cigarette ads, including the Marlboro man, offered an ideal body type and attitude for men—rugged, muscular, and smoking.

dressed in a style similar to the popular Gibson girl of the era. She has an hourglass shape, and the hem of her dress reveals her calves. She holds a pointer as though she is giving a school lesson, and the ad reads: "Duke Cigarettes Are the Best."[52] The product—Duke Cigarettes—was not included in the drawn picture.

While the Duke Cigarette advertisement offered an ideal body type for a woman living in the 1880s, other ads would likewise present the male body type. In an advertisement for Marlboro cigarettes, a man is leaning against a horse saddle in a barn, dressed in jeans, cowboy boots and hat, and Western shirt; he has the slight muscular build of man who works outdoors. Unlike the teacher, however, he is smoking a cigarette, and two

Advertising and Beauty Contests

In 1921 in Atlantic City, New Jersey, a group of community leaders decided on a scheme to promote tourism over Labor Day weekend. The idea was a beauty contest, originally called the Atlantic City Pageant, but later renamed Miss America. While the idea for a beauty pageant was not new, the evolution of the Miss America pageant modernized the idea of a beauty contest by initiating swimsuit and other competitions. The pageant was first televised in 1955 and during the 1960s was one of the highest rated programs on television. Despite the growing popularity of the program, however, social critics wondered whether the Miss America contest truly represented all American women.

The contest rules for Miss America had frequently placed a number of limitations on contestants, including age, height, and weight. For much of the contest's history, limitations were also placed on skin color, and the issue of ethnicity was suppressed. Early Miss America contestants, then, were overwhelmingly white, Anglo-Saxon, and Protestant, a combination commonly referred to as WASP. For this reason, the Miss America contest has often been accused of offering a narrow idea of body image in the United States.

Some believe that the Miss America pageant continues to offer a limited idea of body types.

packs of Marlboro cigarettes are featured in the advertisement. The caption reads: "Come to where the flavor is. Come to Marlboro Country."[53]

Both of these advertisements revealed a trend in advertisers' willingness to use body image to help sell products. Few teachers, however, especially in rural America, would have dressed in a similar fashion; and, as health studies would later reveal, smoking frequently interferes with the robust body image as represented by Western-attired men. Trends that combined body type and commercial products would accelerate with the birth and growth of radio and television, along with the discovery of a new market audience in the 1940s and 1950s.

Teenagers and Tweens

Another trend in advertising within American history would emerge in the 1940s when advertisers discovered that adults were not the only consumers with money to spare. "The marketing of products to teenagers," writes author Alissa Quart, "has existed since the word *teenager* was coined by Madison Avenue in 1941."[54] As adult women had been reading ad copy in *Ladies Home Journal*, young women began reading ad copy in *Seventeen*. As adult men (primarily) had been reading ad copy in *Sports Illustrated*, young men (primarily) would begin reading ad copy in *Sports Illustrated for Kids*. Like advertisements for adults, advertisement content for teenagers in magazines, radio, and television would use body images in an attempt to sell everything from soft drinks to blue jeans to MP3 players.

An even more recent trend in advertising and the display of body image focuses on even younger children, often referred to as the tween market. The Media Awareness Network writes of the tween market: "One of the most important recent developments in advertising to kids has been the defining of a 'tween' market (ages 8 to 12). No longer little children, and not yet teens, tweens are starting to develop their sense of identity and are anxious to cultivate a sophisticated self-image."[55] The cultivation of self-image and body image, many marketing experts believe, revolves around the purchase of items such as clothing, jewelry, and makeup. As with advertising for adults and teenagers, marketers for tweens also rely on body image to help make these products attractive.

DO NOT BLAME ADVERTISERS

"Does anybody ever stop and think that maybe, just maybe, these children who are too skinny, depressed, or fat end up this way for other reasons? I'll answer for you—no, they don't because Barbie is an easy scapegoat; she's plastic."—Macy I., blogger on Teen Ink Raw Web site.

Macy I., "Mattel, McDonald's, Only Scapegoats for Body Image," Teen Ink Raw, February 2, 2009. www.teenink.com/raw/Opinion/article/48325/Mattel-McDonalds-only-scape goats-for-body-image.

Relying on body image in advertising for the teens and tweens market has perhaps been even more controversial than criticisms leveled at advertising for adults. Many social critics believe that advertisers play on teens' and tweens' insecurities to sell products that promise to make the young consumer more attractive. Furthermore, they argue, advertising to tweens and teens bypasses parental oversight. Others argue that tweens and teens are capable of understanding the methods that advertisers use and that buying products to enhance body image builds self-esteem.

Sex Sells: Calvin Klein

While the use of thin models has created controversy over the display of body image during the last ten years, the combination of sexuality and body image has a long history of controversy. Images featuring sex appeal are frequently used to sell everything from shampoo to cars, and like ultrathin models in fashion magazines, much controversy has been generated over the potential for these sexualized advertisements to impact the way men and women think about body image.

Some of the most controversial use of sexualized bodies to sell products has come from the blue jeans industry. "Designer jeans ads, already recognized as the most risqué genre of commercial advertising, opened a new chapter when they began objectifying the

Calvin Klein's racy ads have pushed the boundaries for the presentation of sexuality.

male body,"[56] notes author James Sullivan. Beginning in the 1970s, no industry would be more aggressive in combining sex and advertising than the designer jeans industry. "Sexual suggestion was being used to sell consumer products a century before the designer jeans uproar, when tobacco companies advertised their cigarettes with underdressed, sometimes completely disrobed women in 'classic poses,'" writes Sullivan. Label names like Jordache, Calvin Klein, and Guess were pushing the envelope on what the public would allow in the presentation of body image. "It was the dramatic success of designer jeans that pushed innuendo in advertising to the brink of soft porn."[57]

No jeans manufacturer would court as many controversies as Calvin Klein, and no campaign was more controversial than his series of ads featuring the young model-actress Brooke Shields. In 1981 Klein initiated a campaign combining sex and advertising that would create one of a long string of controversies for the jeans manufacturer. Early advertisements featuring Shields were controversial primarily because she was only fifteen when the series began, and the ads were highly suggestive sexually:

> When Calvin Klein introduced his jeans campaign in 1981, controversy arose over the sexy ads and commercial spots featuring teen star Brooke Shields seducing audience[s] with her provocative "Know what comes between me and my Calvins? Nothing." Three network-owned stations in New York banned the ads. Nevertheless, sales of the expensive jeans jumped nearly 300% following the first wave of commercials."[58]

Brand Names

Because advertising combines body image ideas with products, consumers are frequently led to believe that a specific product can provide the magic key for popularity or the right body type. In *Branded: The Buying and Selling of Teenagers*, Alissa Quart recalls her first experience of believing that a brand name would change her life.

> I remember standing in a changing room at Macy's, trying to figure out how to let my inner coolness out. Would Jordache jeans or Esprit corduroys help me? Given my limited allowance (not enough to afford a matching shirt), I knew I would never be mistaken for one of the normal girls in my class. Those girls had shiny hair and perfect Gloria Vanderbilt jeans and white swans embroidered on the back pockets. I attempted to explain the sportswear semiotics to my mother, an early earthy feminist, and she responded with solicitous confusion. Why were all these pricey things so necessary? she wondered. Why was normality important? The answer, of course, was simple: The Jordache Look!

Alissa Quart, *Branded: The Buying and Selling of Teenagers*. New York: Perseus, 2003, p. xv.

In 1999 many media critics believed that Klein crossed the line with a series of advertisements featuring children dressed in the company's underwear. Of the three ads, two featured two small boys on a sofa wearing only Calvin Klein underwear; a third ad featured two girls, also on a sofa and wearing Calvin Klein underwear. Many critics labeled the ads child pornography, and because of the public outcry against them the ads were pulled within twenty-four hours. Klein apologized for the ads, noting that it had not been his intention to sexualize children's bodies. Nonetheless, author Pamela A. Ivinski notes that advertisers have seemed determined to reach younger and younger audiences: "Soon enough we'll be striving to reach consumers in utero [in the womb]. What more noble pursuit for the designer gene industry?"[59]

Critics of these advertisers accused manufacturers like Klein of sexualizing young bodies, arguing that these advertisements could influence teenage consumers' ideas about body image. Others argue that the influence of these advertisements was overstated. Advertisers were simply selling young consumers the products they wanted and presenting these products in a way designed to capture their attention.

Fashion Magazines and Modeling

One common method of using body image to help sell commercial products to children and adults is the use of models in fashion magazines. Fashion magazines such as *Glamour* and *Elle* feature multiple layouts of models wearing new lines of clothing. While many may think of modeling as primarily a female profession, males also work as models. Male models appear in the same fashion magazines as women, while also appearing in the advertisements of men's magazines like *GQ*.

As with media criticism, a number of controversies have emerged around the issue of whether models affect men's and women's concepts of body image. Some social critics and psychologists believe these models set an unhealthy example. Michelle Lee, a former *Glamour* and *Mademoiselle* editor, writes: "A woman between the ages of 18 and 34 has a 1 percent chance of being as thin as a super model. Nearly 50 percent of all teenage girls in one study said they wanted to lose weight after viewing

Models—seen on television and in advertisements—weigh 23 percent less than the average woman and represent an ideal nearly impossible to achieve.

Bibliotheque Saint-Claude Library

magazines, when only 29 percent were overweight."[60] The Media Awareness Network, a Web site dedicated to media education for young people, notes: "Twenty years ago, the average model weighed 8 percent less than the average woman—but today's models weigh 23 percent less."[61]

Some advertising experts, however, note that the fact that models lead different lives and experience different job demands than the average person is common knowledge. The perfect look, for instance, requires a great deal of effort, and models expend a great deal of time to achieve the perfect look. "Every model must spend hours each day on personal care," writes Halperin. "Cosmetics, skin care, hair care, body care, and fragrances are a daily routine."[62] Understanding these requirements, these critics argue, most people do not expect to look like a model.

Furthermore, models and images of models may be enhanced in a number of ways. Many enhance appearances with cosmetic surgery and liposuction. Photographs of models in magazines are further refined by airbrushing, a process that removes blemishes, cellulite, and other items from the picture. Grogan notes: "Digital manipulations of pictures of models' bodies mean that women in the 2000s are faced with even more idealized, and more slender bodies than in the 1990s."[63] While a number of models are able to maintain the idealized shape featured in many contemporary magazines, studies reveal that women are aware that achieving these images is an unrealistic goal, and many express resentment at models they consider overly thin, such as Kate Moss.

Besides a greater awareness of media, a number of social critics observe, television has also begun to offer reality programs about modeling that feature a number of plus-size models. In 2008 Whitney Thompson became the first plus-size model to win on *America's Next Top Model*. Victories such as this, critics argue, offer a more balanced view of body image within the media and advertising.

The Thin Line Between Ads and Entertainment

Part of the dilemma of using body images within advertisements is that while advertisements are designed to sell products, they are also frequently designed to entertain the viewer. Graydon, in her book *Made You Look: How Advertising Works and Why You Should Know*, suggests that some television programming may, in fact, be advertising.

Graydon focuses this criticism on music videos as frequently seen on television stations like MTV (Music Television) and CMT (Country Music Television). "Music videos can be very expensive to make, but recording companies give them to TV stations free," Graydon writes. "They know that every time a music video is aired, it's like a three- or four-minute commercial for the performer's CD."[64] In this case, watching a video on MTV or CMT would be the same as watching a commercial: The video is designed to sell a CD, while commercials are designed to sell other products. Both use attractive body images to help sell a product.

Does Advertising Affect Attitudes About Body Image?

The basic idea behind most advertising is to capture a consumer's attention and then convince the consumer to buy the featured product. Many advertisers seem to believe that using body images helps to accomplish this goal. The desire for advertisers to sell products, however, may reveal little about how advertisers utilize body image ideals to reach that goal. In a basic sense, media observers generalize, the psychology of advertisements appeal to men's and women's common desires: Most people wish to be attractive, and advertising seems to offer the promise that they will be attractive if they purchase a particular product.

Other advertising critics, however, note that besides appealing to common desires, some advertising may play upon people's insecurities about body image. "Growing up in a social context in which models' bodies are used to sell products and lifestyles and atmospheres," notes Quart, "teenagers feel significant pressure to purchase whatever it takes to become part of that role."[65] In the scenario, the advertiser may imply that the body image of a boy or girl will be deficient unless he or she purchases a specific brand of clothing or makeup. Studies relating to how advertising affects personal concepts of body image, and how long the effects of advertising remain, are inconclusive.

Finally, a number of social critics have noted that while the use of body image may be prevalent in advertising, people still retain a great deal of control over the number and kinds of images they will see each day. While it may be difficult to completely avoid advertising in daily life, individuals can choose whether or not to read fashion magazines or watch television or surf the net.

BODY IMAGE AND OBSESSION

In the mid-1990s Johnston recognized that it was normal for men and women to express concern over appearance. "It's a fact that physical attractiveness is prized in our culture," writes Johnston. "There is nothing wrong with wanting to 'look good.'"[66] In contemporary culture, however, a number of social critics like Johnston believe that concern over appearance has become excessive. The excessive, many argue, has the potential to lead to a number of related problems connected to body image issues. Johnston has suggested that appearance is so much in focus today that it has become an obsession. Kate Fox, writing for the Social Issues Research Centre, agrees with Johnston: "We are all more obsessed with our appearance than we like to admit. But this is not an indication of 'vanity.' Vanity means conceit, excessive pride in one's appearance. Concern about appearance is quite normal and understandable. Attractive people have distinct advantages in our society."[67]

An example of this obsession might be dieting. Social observers have noted that dieting has become a common topic at work, school, and home, and popular diets—from South Beach to Atkins—have multiplied. Gyms and health centers have also multiplied, and membership continues to increase. Disturbing signs of appearance obsession become more obvious, however, when dieting and exercise focus less on healthy lifestyle choices than on achieving the perfect body. While more men and women diet, more of them seem to be developing eating disorders; while more men and women exercise, more of them seem to be developing exercise-related disorders. Johnston writes: "When we are appearance obsessed, we constantly diet, exercise compulsively and rely on fashion to soothe, temporarily, the perpetual dissatisfaction we feel about our bodies and looks."[68]

While statistics may not prove a connection between body image concerns and eating or exercise disorders, they do reveal these disorders as common occurrences in contemporary society. In a 2003 study, researchers H.W. Hoek and D. van Hoeken published the following statistics:

- 40% of newly identified cases of anorexia are in girls fifteen to nineteen years old

- Significant increase in incidence of anorexia from 1935 to 1989 especially among young women fifteen to twenty-four

- A rise in incidence of anorexia in young women fifteen to nineteen in each decade since 1930

- The incidence of bulimia in ten- to thirty-nine year old women tripled between 1988 and 1993

- Only one-third of people with anorexia in the community receive mental health care

- Only 6% of people with bulimia receive mental health care

- The majority of people with severe eating disorders do not receive adequate care[69]

While many social commentators have blamed the media and advertising for this hyper-focus on body image and the prevalence of eating disorders, there are no easy answers to understanding the reasons for this new focus. Whatever the reasons, hyperfocus on the body and body image has become a major social concern, potentially impacting the health and well-being of millions of people.

Obesity Epidemic

In recent years physicians and popular commentators have drawn attention to a growing population—both in the United States and around the world—of obese adults. Many have referred to this change as an "obesity epidemic." Generally speaking, anyone who weighs more than 10 percent of their healthy weight is overweight; anyone who weighs over 30 percent of their healthy weight is considered obese. A number of researchers add another category called morbid obesity, signifying those who weigh 50 percent to 100 percent over their healthy weight. According to the World Health Organization, over 1 billion adults in the world are overweight, 300 million of whom qualify as obese.

The number of children who are overweight and obese has also grown. The World Health Organization estimates that worldwide, 22 million children are overweight, and the U.S. surgeon general has estimated that the number of overweight children in the United States has tripled since 1980. In the United States, at least 15 percent of those under eighteen are considered overweight. Likewise, the occurrence of obesity in children has continued to grow around the world, including China and Thailand.

A number of reasons has been given for these changes. For many people around the world, access to food, including foods rich in fats and sugars, is more readily available than at any time in human history. The availability of food is further complicated by less physically active lifestyles. As opposed to working all day on a farm as many Americans did during the 1800s, many work in an office behind a desk. "Moves towards less physical activity," notes the World Health Organization, "are also found in the increasing use of automated transport, technology in the home, and more passive leisure pursuits."[70]

The obesity epidemic has also had an important impact on body image. One recent study by the Columbia University Mailman School of Public Health notes the relation between body image ideas and the growing obesity epidemic. Says Peter Muennig, assistant professor of health policy and management at Mailman, "Our data suggest that some of the obesity epidemic may be partially attributable to social constructs that surround ideal body types. Younger persons, whites, and women are disproportionately affected by negative body image concerns, and these groups unduly suffer from BMI [body mass index]-associated morbidity and mortality."[71] Other research suggests that psychological disorders such as depression potentially contribute to obesity. Because of this epidemic and because of the health-related problems including heart trouble and diabetes, the increase in obesity has also focused greater attention on bodies and as a result, more attention on body image.

Dieting

An increase in dieting has mirrored the rise in obesity. Dieting is a widespread phenomenon in contemporary culture and is perhaps the most widely used method of controlling body weight and shape. "Keeping to a diet is a serious component of modern culture,"[72] notes author Peter N. Stearns. Dieting is also very popular in Western cultures. One British study reported that 86 per-

Pictured are various types of diets, including the Zone diet and the Atkins diet. The number of people dieting has increased dramatically worldwide.

cent of all English women have dieted and other studies suggest that as many as 80 percent of girls under the age of thirteen have also dieted. Men also diet but in fewer numbers. In one survey reported by the BBC, it was noted "Almost two in five (37%) women were dieting most of the time, compared to around just one in six (18%) of men."[73]

In the most basic sense, dieting is regulating the intake of food and calories but may also include supplemental vitamins, diet pills, and laxatives. For some people, a diet may consist of no more than skipping meals or limiting fatty foods and desserts. Others may limit proteins or carbohydrates or substitute a diet product like Slim-Fast for one or more regular meals. In extreme cases, dieters reduce calorie intake to a thousand calories or less per day.

Because dieting has become both popular and common, diet aids, books, and supplements have grown into a multibillion-dollar industry. Rebecca Reisner, an editor at *BusinessWeek*, noted in 2008, "Americans spend $40 billion a year on weight-loss programs and products."[74] The names of diets themselves, such as Atkins and South Beach, are familiar and research suggests that the diet industry is one of the fastest-growing industries in the United States. Unfortunately, few dieters seem to obtain the slim body style promised by the weight-loss industry and diets are seldom successful. For obese dieters, success rates have been measured as high as 25 percent; for non-obese dieters, however, success rates are as low as 5 percent.

Worse, dieting can become problematic. Many men and women return to old eating habits after losing weight; then after regaining the weight they diet again. The diet, non-diet routine becomes circular and has been popularly referred to as yo-yo dieting. Another problem is that low-calorie and what is referred to as fad diets may excessively limit calories, depriving the dieter of needed nutrition. These diets may even be counterproductive to losing weight. "Fad diets generally rely on some trick to give the readers the appearance of novelty,"[75] note researchers Dana K. Cassell and David H. Gleaves. Commonly, a person's metabolism will slow down, causing one's body to react as though the dieter were starving. In this state, the body burns fewer calories and will

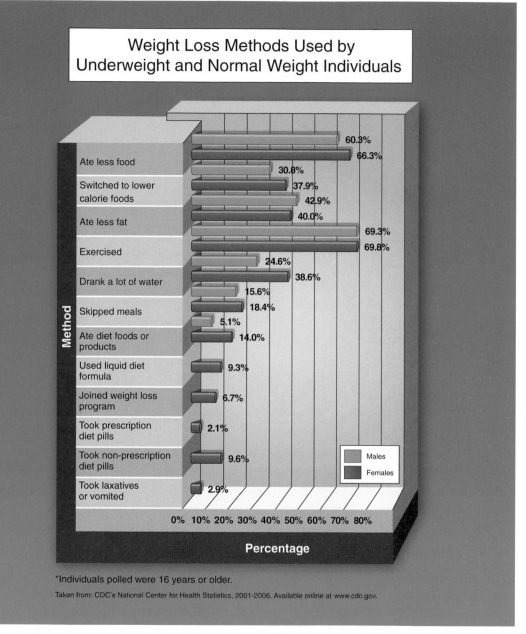

Weight Loss Methods Used by Underweight and Normal Weight Individuals

Method	Males	Females
Ate less food	60.3%	66.3%
Switched to lower calorie foods	30.8%	37.9%
Ate less fat	42.9%	40.0%
Exercised	69.3%	69.8%
Drank a lot of water	24.6%	38.6%
Skipped meals	15.6%	18.4%
Ate diet foods or products	5.1%	14.0%
Used liquid diet formula	9.3%	
Joined weight loss program	6.7%	
Took prescription diet pills	2.1%	
Took non-prescription diet pills	9.6%	
Took laxatives or vomited	2.9%	

Percentage

*Individuals polled were 16 years or older.

Taken from: CDC's National Center for Health Statistics, 2001-2006. Available online at www.cdc.gov.

frequently burn both fat and muscle. When the person quits dieting, he or she frequently gains weight more quickly as the body seeks to replenish what it has lost during starvation mode. In the worst case scenario, dieting may even lead to eating disorders.

Eating Disorders

Eating disorders are potential side effects of dieting, especially with yo-yo and other unhealthy fad diets. Many sociologists and researchers believe that these disorders often are associated with concern over body image, especially for children and young adults. "At a time when they should feel secure in their body's growth, too many American children become anxious about size and weight and begin to eat in ways that contribute to the very problems they hope to avoid," notes psychotherapist Kathy Kater. "Obesity, negative body image, and eating disorders are extremely difficult to reverse once established, and can be devastating to the self-esteem of developing bodies and egos."[76]

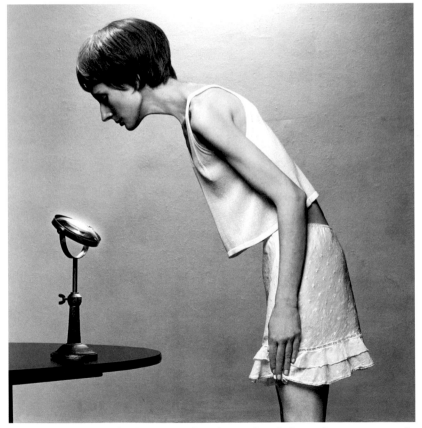

Poor body image can lead to eating disorders such as bulimia, binge eating, and anorexia (seen here).

While doctors have been familiar with eating disorders since the end of the 1800s, the broader public did not become aware of the wide range of eating disorders, including binge eating, anorexia nervosa, and bulimia, until the 1970s and 1980s. Public recognition of eating disorders followed the death of Karen Carpenter, the popular singing member of the Carpenters duo. She died of heart failure brought on by anorexia in 1983. "Because of her popularity," write Cassell and Gleaves, "her death brought more attention to eating disorders than anything before or since."[77] While the underlying causes of eating disorders are varied, ranging from low self-esteem to social anxiety, all feature a hyperconcern for body shape and image. According to the National Institutes of Health, anorexia, bulimia, and binge eating are considered mental disorders.

Substantiating statistics on eating disorders is difficult, primarily because most people who suffer from eating disorders wish to keep this information private. In the case of anorexia, the severe weight loss eventually becomes obvious. Still, it is unclear

Living with Anorexia

In Audrey Shehyn's *Picture This: Young Women Speak Their Minds,* seventeen-year-old Candice talks about her struggles with food:

> Weight has been a big thing. I've been on a diet since I was in fourth grade. My Mom says I probably always will be. Last year at this time, I probably weighed twenty-five pounds more. I'm still not content with my body, but my things fit me better and I don't get called names anymore.

If someone's going to put you down that's the first thing they go to, if you are overweight. Last year, there was this guy who was really mean to me; he'd always call me "fat." I'd go home and cry about it, even stay home from school to avoid it for one day. When you're overweight, you know it and you don't need to be told it by someone else.

Audrey Shehyn, *Picture This: Young Women Speak Their Minds.* New York: Hyperion, 2000, pp. 148–49.

if everyone who suffers the symptoms of anorexia can technically be referred to as anorexic: As many as one-third of anorexics have been described by researchers as me-too anorexics, meaning that these individuals are simply copying the behavior of friends or classmates.

Binge eating may seem easier to identify because of weight gain, but this physical change is misleading: Not all obese people are binge eaters. Finally, bulimia may be the most difficult eating disorder of all to detect. While bulimia most often begins in a person's teens or early twenties, it is seldom discovered until the bulimic is in her thirties or forties. Since bulimia is so difficult to detect, and because bulimia is much more common than anorexia, overall statistics on eating disorders remain difficult to validate. Author Joan Jacobs Bromberg nonetheless argues that these eating disorders should be taken seriously: "The annual incidence of the disorder [anorexia nervosa] has never been estimated at more than 1.6 per 100,000 population. Still, among adolescent girls and young women there is an increasing and disturbing amount of anorexia nervosa and bulimia."[78]

Anorexia Nervosa, Binge Eating Disorder (BED), and Bulimia

Translated literally, *anorexia* means "not hungry" or "without an appetite." The literal definition, however, is misleading, because anorexics are frequently hungry. Anorexics fear gaining weight and limit their calorie intake to as little as possible to maintain thinness. Helpguide.org defines anorexia as:

- Refusal to sustain a minimally normal body weight

- Intense fear of gaining weight, despite being underweight

- Distorted view of one's body or weight, or denial of the dangers of one's low weight[79]

Even when anorexics appear thin to others, they frequently continue to see themselves as heavier. Even when anorexics become emaciated, they are often proud of this accomplishment. Traditionally, incidences of anorexia were limited to primarily

Anorexia and Boys

In Sherry S. Handel's *Blue Jean: What Young Women Are Thinking, Saying, and Doing*, thirteen-year-old Jacquelyn Motonian wanted to discover "The Other Side of the Mirror": What was it like when boys became anorexic? To find out, Motonian spoke to Dan Long, a man who had been anorexic as a high school student.

> Dan said he never felt that he was fat, but that he was afraid of getting fat. "I felt what triggered my anorexia was the transition from high school to college. I wrestled for a sport, and I felt I always needed to be the same weight as my opponent. If he was lighter than I was, I lost the weight by exercising. On the other hand, if he was heavier, I exercised more and ate less to try to gain more muscle."
>
> He shared a very disturbing secret: "Even when I took a shower, the water would hurt my back because there was nothing to protect my bones except skin." Dan told me that he wasn't diagnosed until he was only 125 pounds. "My parents got me psychological help," he said. "I went twice a week. The doctor I went to had never worked with a male, so he was giving me advice that I didn't need. That was when I realized that men and women get anorexia for different reasons."

Sherry S. Handel, *Blue Jean: What Young Women Are Thinking, Saying, and Doing*. Rochester, NY: Blue Jean, 2001, pp. 171–72.

white, affluent teenagers, though this has changed recently. Statistics estimate between 1 percent and 2 percent of adolescent and young adult women suffer from anorexia, though the estimate rises to as high as one in ten for female college students. "Many anorexics go through periods of bingeing and purging as well, which puts additional stress on their bodies,"[80] writes Yancey.

In reducing calorie intake, anorexics frequently damage their health, leading to as many as fifteen deaths per hundred patients treated for the disease. While treatment is often successful, as many as half of anorexics suffer relapses.

Binge eating disorder (BED) is defined as people who eat massive portions of food at least twice a week and typically do not compensate for this behavior by purging (or vomiting) or using laxatives. Frequently binge eaters become overweight. "Compulsive overeaters are also overweight," writes Yancey, "but they may overeat all the time rather than binge."[81]

Bulimia may almost seem like the opposite of anorexia, but the desired result—a lower body weight and a more desired body image—is the same. While bulimics also binge, they compensate by vomiting or taking laxatives to expunge calories from their bodies. Like anorexia, bulimia frequently begins during the teenage years and is highlighted by a hyper-concern over body shape and size.

Binge eating disorder (BED) is when people eat massive portions of food but do not purge as bulimics do.

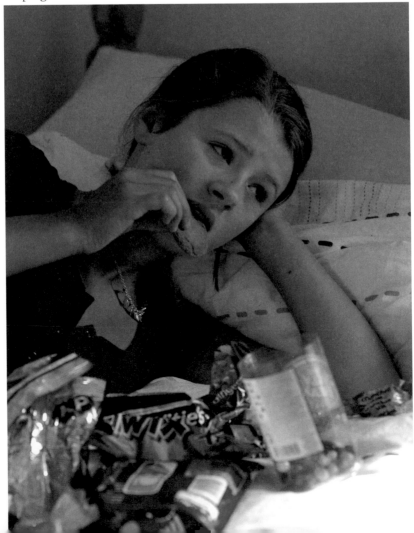

ANOREXIA AND BULIMIA ARE NOT THE REAL PROBLEM

"It turns out that for a long time now, parents have so worried that these waif-adoring times would drive their teens to self-starvation that they have missed the real threat—the steady fattening of America's young."—H.J. Cummins, journalist, author, and editor.

H.J. Cummins, "A Minor Problem of Size," *Star Tribune* (Minneapolis-St. Paul, MN), December 8, 1997. www.highbeam.com/doc/1G1-62620631.html.

The disorder often begins with experimental, self-induced vomiting to get rid of unwanted calories," writes Yancey, "then quickly becomes a terrible compulsion."[82] Statistics point to the fact that bulimia is much more common than anorexia, affecting as many as 4 percent or 5 percent of the adolescent/young adult female population.

Exercise and Bodybuilding

Broadly speaking, exercise covers a wide range of activities designed to improve health and fitness through physical activity. Because exercise and sports help burn fat calories, many people also exercise to lose weight or maintain a healthy weight. Likewise, exercise helps tone and shape the body, leading men and women to exercise for an enhanced body image. Because bodies process calories more slowly as people grow older, exercise also balances the gradual weight gain that sometimes occurs as they reach middle age.

While the benefits of exercise are generally thought of as positive and healthy, it can become an obsession. Exercise obsession equals overexercising and is often pursued to achieve a desired body shape and to enhance a body part (muscular arms, a flat stomach, and so forth). Men and women who jog excessively, for instance, may damage knees or other body parts. "Too much exercise and the body breaks down physically," writes author Michelle Biton. "Bones suffer, as do tendons, ligaments, even muscles."[83] Exercise obsession is also common in people who have eating disorders: Exercise is used to burn off unwanted calories. "Breaking an exercise addiction can be as difficult as overcoming an eating disorder,"[84] note Cassell and Gleaves.

Bodybuilding is a type of exercise that involves lifting weights at home, school, or at a health club. As with general exercise, bodybuilding is used to enhance body shape and self-esteem. Bodybuilding has generally been seen as a male-oriented sport, promoting more muscular body types. "Bodybuilding is becoming more and more popular worldwide as a way for men to attain the culturally valued slender, muscular body,"[85] writes Grogan. Over time, however, bodybuilding has also become more popular with women, though women bodybuilders may face social obstacles by attempting to achieve a body style that is less socially acceptable. "Bodybuilding is not generally seen as appropriate for women, and women who engage in this sport may face discrimination,"[86] writes Grogan. As with men, women have their own bodybuilding competitions.

Bodybuilding, like exercise in general, has a number of health benefits if practiced responsibly. When taken to extremes, however, bodybuilding may result in a number of unhealthy side effects. One particular danger has been the use of anabolic steroids to help build greater muscle mass. The use of steroids can have serious side effects, including liver damage, hypertension (high blood pressure), and kidney damage; and the hypodermic needles that are frequently used by athletes to inject steroids may possibly spread infectious diseases such as AIDS. Many of the side effects of steroids affect men and women differently. In women, steroids may cause baldness, breast reduction, the growth of body hair, and the deepening of voice; in men, steroids may cause infertility and the growth of breasts. For adolescents, the use of steroids may stunt the development of bone structure, especially if taken before a growth spurt.

Body Dysmorphic Disorder (BDD) and the Adonis Complex

While excessive dieting and exercise may represent a desire to alter one's overall body image, body dysmorphic disorder focuses on an obsession with an imagined or mentally magnified body

Bodybuilding has a number of health benefits but can have dangerous side effects if practiced irresponsibly.

defect. The Mayo Clinic notes that body dysmorphic disease has also been called "imagined ugliness." It is common for those with BDD to focus on one or more body parts as unsatisfactory, typically the face, body hair, skin blemishes, thighs, breasts, and buttocks. A person suffering from BDD may be distressed and normal functioning may be impaired. BDD is estimated to occur in 1 percent to 2 percent of the world's population and is equally common in women and men. The Mayo Clinic lists a number of symptoms:

- Preoccupation with your physical appearance

- Strong belief that you have an abnormality or defect in your appearance that makes you ugly

- Frequently examining yourself in the mirror or, conversely, avoiding mirrors altogether

- Believing that others take special notice of your appearance in a negative way

- Frequent cosmetic procedures with little satisfaction

- Excessive grooming, such as hair plucking

- Feeling extremely self-conscious

- Refusing to appear in pictures

- Skin picking

- Comparing your appearance with that of others

- Avoiding social situations

- Wearing excessive makeup or clothing to camouflage perceived flaws[87]

Like eating disorders, BDD is most often developed in adolescence or young adulthood and may be accompanied by depression and social phobia and in some cases may include the symptoms of suicidal tendencies. It is commonly believed that people suffering from BDD are self-centered or vain, though the opposite is often true: People with BDD obsess about their appearance because they believe they are ugly.

The Adonis Complex, also referred to as reverse anorexia and muscle dysmorphia, is a specific type of body dysmorphic disorder. "Nowadays, it seems, increasing numbers of boys and men . . . have become fixated on achieving a perfect, Adonis-like body,"[88] notes researchers Harrison G. Pope Jr., Katherine A. Phillips, and Roberto Olivardia. With the Adonis Complex, boys and men (primarily) become obsessed with whether they are muscular enough, and this may lead to excessive exercise and other obsessive behavior. "Research from the USA shows that many body-builders think they are puny," notes writer David Batty. "At its most extreme, this is known as muscle dysmorphia or 'bigorexia' (reverse anorexia)."[89]

EATING DISORDERS ARE DANGEROUS

"Eating disorders can be life threatening. Young people with anorexia nervosa, for example, have difficulty maintaining a minimum healthy body weight. Anorexia affects one in every 100 to 200 adolescent girls and a much smaller number of boys."—National Mental Health Information Center.

National Mental Health Information Center, "Children's Mental Health Facts: Children and Adolescents with Mental, Emotional, and Behavioral Disorders," February 2, 2009. http://mentalhealth.samhsa.gov/publications/allpubs/CA-0006/default.asp.

Many with the Adonis complex rely on diet supplements along with anabolic steroids to improve muscle mass. "For many of the muscle-bound men and women identified as having the disorder," notes *Doctor's Guide*, "preoccupation with their bodies was so intense they routinely gave up desirable jobs, careers and social engagements to spend hours in a gym each day."[90]

ALTERING BODY IMAGE

In the twenty-first century, physically altering one's body to enhance appearance has become common in Western cultures. These alterations range from tattoos and piercings to liposuction and plastic surgery. While these processes can be traced back to long-standing cultural traditions in many countries, today they have taken on new meaning in relation to enhancement of body image. These trends are partly driven by two changes: One, attitudes toward physically altering one's body have become more socially acceptable; and two, the processes have become affordable to the middle class. In this environment, spending money for cosmetic surgery may even be considered a sign of prestige.

These physical alterations, like dieting and exercise, are intertwined with personal identity and body image development. When a boy or girl decides to enhance body image with a piercing or tattoo, these decisions—the design of the tattoo and the body part that will be pierced—may be used to display a person's individuality. In many cases, these behaviors may also mark a rite of passage. "They [experts] argue that because our culture doesn't provide such rituals . . .," notes Graydon, "kids have to make up their own."[91] In other cases, these acts may also qualify as a form of rebellion. Whether these cosmetic processes represent identity issues or rebellion, they provide multiple ways for people to enhance and alter body image.

In one sense, physical alterations of the body have been available in some forms (such as tattoos) throughout most of human history. The difference today, social observers have noted, is the sheer variety of processes. In many contemporary developed

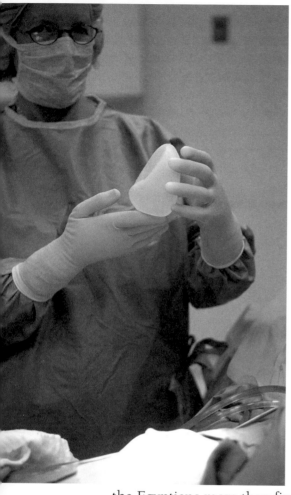

Physical alterations, including breast implants, are intertwined with personal identity.

countries such as Canada, the average middle-class man or woman can enhance or alter his or her body image with tattoos, liposuction, Botox, body piercing, and plastic surgery. All of these procedures and the debates that surround them continue to impact ideas about body image.

Tattoos and Body Piercing

Historically, tattooing is an ancient art and has been practiced in many parts of the world. For thousands of years, men and women have painted, tattooed, and pierced their bodies to enhance body image and attractiveness. "Tattooing is one of the ancient body arts," notes author Julian Robinson, "known to the Egyptians more than five thousand years ago."[92] In contemporary societies, tattooing is usually accomplished with needles that inject dye into the top layer of skin. Tattoos are semipermanent, come in multiple designs and colors, and can be either etched in easily displayed parts of the body or hidden from public view.

In contemporary Western cultures, practices of body decorating have changed dramatically during the last twenty-five to fifty years. Having one's ears pierced and wearing decorative earrings, for example, has been common, though primarily practiced by women until the 1970s and more recently, by some homosexual males. Likewise, until recently tattoos were mostly worn by cultural subgroups including prisoners, members of gangs, and circus performers. When practiced by a subgroup, body decorating has often served as a shortcut for identifying other members of the group while also separating the group from mainstream society.

Today, however, many of these associations have been lost, and people consider body art as another way to decorate themselves. "Tattooing and body piercing have become popular with people of all ages, occupations, and social classes, and have become mainstream and acceptable across the social spectrum, at least for the

Tattooing is an ancient art that has been practiced all over the world.

Tattoos

Once, tattoos were uncommon in mainstream society, and many associated those who wore tattoos as prisoners, sailors, and members of motorcycle gangs. Women seldom wore tattoos. Today, as Silja J.A. Talvi's story recounts, tattoos have become common for men and women from all sections of society.

To be sure, tattooing is not a decision to be made lightly or half-heartedly. But when such a decision is made, it typically marks an important stage in a woman's life—a process of discovering, exploring and learning on the very surface of the body.

Many women seek out tattoos for altogether joyful reasons—to celebrate ethnic, spiritual or cultural heritages; to mark exciting life transitions or to display a lifelong beautification. To dismiss tattoos as a form of self-oppression is to miss out on the fascinating complexity behind each woman's decision to adorn her body with one or more permanent designs. Much of the time, tattoos on a woman truly say something about her character, her life and her spirit.

Ophira Edut, ed., *Adios Barbie: Young Women Write About Body Image and Identity*. Washington, DC: Seal, 1998, pp. 214–15.

young,"[93] notes Grogan. Whereas body art once helped to separate different subgroups from the mainstream, today it may serve as a social shortcut to inclusion in the mainstream.

As tattoos and body piercing have become more popular in recent years in Western cultures, the shape and variety of procedures have multiplied. Body piercing has moved from earlobes to tongues, lips, noses, belly buttons, and nipples, while tattoos are frequently placed on the lower back, calves, and upper arms. "Body art has become so popular in the past few years," notes the Internet site Kids Health, "that it's hard to walk down the street, go to the mall, or watch TV without seeing someone with a piercing or a tattoo."[94] Body piercing is less permanent than tattooing, because once the ring or body jewelry is removed, the skin usually grows over the piercing. Tattoos can be removed, though the procedure may be painful.

Many of these decorating practices revolve around body image and individual style. "My tattoos are an affirmation of my cultural independence," one tattoo wearer told Robinson. "You have them carried out on your body in the full knowledge that this is your body to have and enjoy while you're here."[95] Likewise, the style and body area of the alteration may be important. "The site of piercing and tattoos may be crucial in determining the culture meaning associated with both,"[96] notes Grogan.

Collagen, Botox, and Liposuction

While tattoos and piercing help adorn the body and enhance body image, they do little to address concerns such as body weight and the effects of aging. Collagen, Botox, and liposuction, on the other hand, promise to make men and women thinner and reduce the effects of wrinkles caused by the aging process. All of these procedures are fairly new, dating back no further than the 1970s for collagen, the 1980s for liposuction, and the 1990s for Botox. All of these procedures have become extremely popular methods of enhancing body image.

Despite the risks, liposuction has become a popular procedure for both men and women.

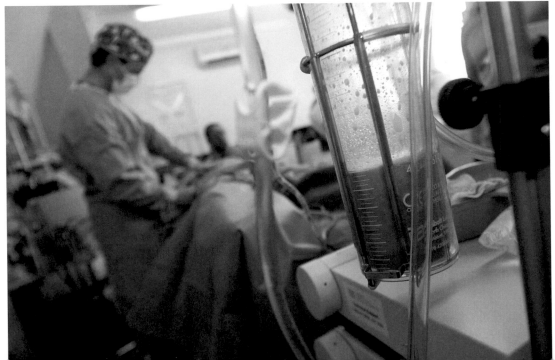

The injected variety of collagen is derived from cow skin, one of many products injected into the face to smooth wrinkles and to plump lips. The collagen is combined with an anesthetic such as lidocaine, mixed into a paste, and then injected into the desired area. An injection costs approximately four hundred dollars and lasts from two weeks to six months, at which time another injection is needed to achieve the same effect. Botox, a botulinum toxin type A bacterium, is used to similar effect. Botox works by paralyzing facial muscles that cause wrinkling, and the effects usually last between three and four months. Taken over a period of time, the effect of Botox may remain even without injections. In 2005, 221,000 collagen and 3.3 million Botox injections were administered in the United States. Allergan, the manufacturer of Botox, sold $831 million of its product the same year.

Liposuction is a process by which plastic surgeons remove fat from beneath the skin. "No procedure exemplifies the Hollywood image of the plastic surgeon more than liposuction,"[97] notes sur-

Male Breast Reduction

It is not uncommon for boys and young men to develop breasts, an occurrence that often leads to social teasing. The Ohio State University Medical Center estimates that most cases of gynecomastia or breast enlargement occur during puberty and affect as many as 65 percent of fourteen-year-old boys. In the majority of these cases, these hormonal changes pose no problem; in 90 percent of the cases, these hormonal changes are eventually outgrown. In a small number of cases, however, breast reduction surgery becomes an option. In 2007 approximately 23,670 boys and men had breast reduction or gynecomastia surgery. A young man from Britain recalls his surgery:

"I wasn't guilty about changing myself—I was glad the damn things were gone. . . . I'm not sure if no longer possessing moobs [male breasts] has had a huge impact on my love life, bar my own image of myself naked, which is obviously much improved. But what I am convinced of is that it's made me a more presentable and confident professional."

Steve Beale, "How I Got Rid of My 'Moobs,'" *Times*, February 5, 2007. www.timesonline.co.uk/tol/life_and_style/men/article1334483.ece.

geon Arthur W. Perry. In 2008, 341,144 liposuction surgeries were performed, and the procedure is popular with men and women. The procedure requires one or more incisions in the skin and the insertion of a hollow tube connected to a liposuction machine. Small incisions are made in less visible sections of the body, and a local anesthesia such as lidocaine is used. "Because our culture is so critical of people who are overweight," writes Graydon, "you can understand why an operation that can get rid of fat overnight—no dieting or exercise necessary—is appealing."[98]

All of these products, if handled professionally, often deliver the advertised results, magically ridding men and women of unwanted fat along with unwanted wrinkles. In essence, they offer a method of enhancing one's body image and personal identity by seemingly preserving a youthful appearance. Each process, however, does have drawbacks and potential hazards. Many people are allergic to collagen, and some argue that collagen may make the face appear unnatural. Botox is less likely to create an allergic reaction, though it too, by paralyzing muscles, may reduce the expressive range of the face. While liposuction has become less dangerous since the 1980s, a number of potential problems still occur, including excessive bleeding.

Surgery and Body Image

Modern reconstructive and cosmetic surgery date back to the mid-1800s, first used to restructure noses (rhinoplasty) and later to reshape ears and breasts. Beginning in the 1900s, the field grew rapidly, partly because of the experience that surgeons gained with injured soldiers during periods of war. "While many advances were made through the ages further perfecting and adding to the specialty," note authors Richard Backstein and Anna Hinek, "medical historians generally consider the modern specialty of plastic surgery to have emerged during the First World War."[99]

By the 1960s cosmetic surgery had become popular with Hollywood stars and the wealthy; by the 1980s new techniques allowed the field of cosmetic surgery to grow; and by the 1990s cosmetic surgery had been embraced by the middle class in developed nations like the United States and Great Britain. "Surgery can change one's appearance into something that nature never intended: bigger breasts, bigger lips, a smaller nose, less fat around the thighs,"[100] writes Perry.

THE PSYCHOLOGICAL BENEFITS OF PLASTIC SURGERY ARE UNKNOWN

"Studies have shown that people report increased satisfaction with the body part they had surgery on, but results are mixed on whether plastic surgery boosts their self-esteem, quality of life, self-confidence and interpersonal relationships in the long term."—Melissa Dittmann, staff writer for the American Psychological Association's *Monitor* magazine.

Melissa Dittmann, "Plastic Surgery: Beauty or Beast?" *Monitor on Psychology*, September 8, 2005. www.apa.org/monitor/sep05/surgery.html.

Both reconstructive surgery and cosmetic surgery alter the body. Theoretically, "reconstructive surgery" applies to repairing body trauma from a car accident, disease, or war and is generally seen as medically necessary; "cosmetic surgery" applies to any improvement or change in a person's appearance. In reality, however, these categories are difficult to separate, partly because both alter the body and thus involve body image. "One hundred fifty years ago it was difficult to separate the two fields, and it's still tough today,"[101] writes Perry. Doctors also argue that cosmetic surgery may be important for some patients' psychological health.

The other big changes in reconstructive and cosmetic surgery are cost, accessibility, and social acceptance of the procedures. "As cosmetic surgery has become more universally accepted," writes author Jan Willis, "the costs have been controlled and it is now available to people across most social and economical lines."[102] This has allowed the general population greater flexibility in changing any physical feature they dislike, such as a nose, or correcting a physical liability, such as a clubfoot. This power to make alterations, many surgeons believe, enhances individual self-esteem and improves overall body image.

Reconstructive Surgery

Reconstructive surgery is generally considered to be the opposite of cosmetic surgery—a necessity rather than only cosmetically desirable. Reconstructive surgery involves repairing bodies that have experienced trauma and is the oldest kind of plastic surgery. "In World War II," writes Graydon, "soldiers were coming back from the European front with their faces so damaged that they were unrecognizable. Surgeons, in addition to trying to save their lives, did everything they could to patch up their faces."[103] Many innovations in reconstructive surgery continue to be connected to war.

Dr. Ali Bayrakdar, a specialist in reconstructive surgery, performs an operation in Baghdad, Iraq, in 2004. Reconstructive surgeons often work with soldiers, cancer patients, and accident victims.

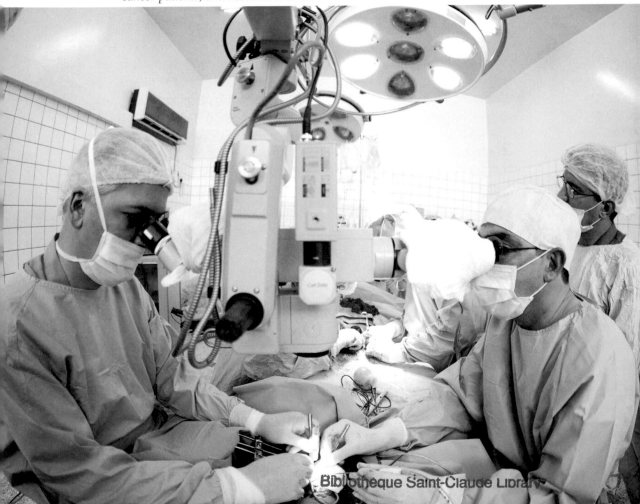

Bibliotheque Saint-Claude Library

"Clearly, the devastation of war was the catalyst that propelled the field of plastic surgery on the path to its current global prominence,"[104] note Backstein and Hinek. Besides war, reconstructive surgery may involve working with men and women who have had cancer, been in an accident, or had tumors removed.

A very basic benefit of reconstructive surgery revolves around self-image and body image. While everyone's body changes over time, these changes are usually subtle, allowing the person to psychologically adjust to these changes. In the case of body trauma from war or surgery, however, the individual may find it difficult to adjust to sudden changes. Reconstructive surgery helps an individual adjust to these changes by making the body look more like it did before the trauma.

One common procedure is breast reconstruction, commonly performed after mastectomies, the removal of part or the entire breast, usually from breast cancer. The surgeon forms a replacement from silicone or saline, and the reconstruction can sometimes be completed in unison with the mastectomies. According to *Cancer Weekly*, 57,100 breast reconstructions were completed in 2007. While many believe that breast implants can have a positive psychological impact leading to an improved body image, they also have several drawbacks. The reconstructed breast has no feeling, and it seldom lasts for a lifetime, potentially requiring more surgery at a later date. Despite these drawbacks, a recent survey in the United States reported that the majority of women receiving the surgery were happy with the results.

Cosmetic Surgery

While men and women may be unable to change basic physical features such as how tall they are, cosmetic surgery promises the next best thing: a chance to radically alter their appearance by redesigning a number of their features. A multitude of procedures are available: brow-lifts, eyelid lifts, and face lifts; breast enlargement, lifts, or reduction; tummy tucks and spider vein removal. Cosmetic surgeons may even be looked upon as artists, shaping the contours of the body into a more perfect alignment. "How you look alters others' perceptions of you," writes Perry. "Like it or not, more attractive people have a lot of advantages in life."[105]

Throughout the 1990s and 2000s more and more people chose to have cosmetic surgery. According to the American Society of Aesthetic Plastic Surgery, "The top five surgical cosmetic procedures in 2008 were: breast augmentation (355,671 procedures); liposuction (341,144 procedures); eyelid surgery (195,104 procedures); rhinoplasty (152,434 procedures); and abdominoplasty (147,392 procedures)."[106] The popularity of cosmetic surgery is also reflected in television programs like *Extreme Makeover*, *The Swan*, and *Nip/Tuck*. While women have cosmetic surgery at much higher rates than men, men are also developing new attitudes toward cosmetic surgery. "Men are increasingly likely to have cosmetic surgery to change the way they look,"[107] notes Grogan.

PLASTIC SURGERY HELPS SELF-ESTEEM

"Plastic surgery was once reserved for the rich and famous, but is now more affordable and safe. All surgery has risks, but the benefits can sometimes far outweigh the potential problems. I have seen plastic surgery dramatically improve people's lives, physically and emotionally."—Shahin Javaheri, plastic surgeon.

Shahin Javaheri, "Cosmetic Surgery Can Boost Self-Image," *Contra Costa Times*, August 17, 2007. www.cchealth.org/topics/column/healthy_outlook_aug17_2007.php.

Many people choose cosmetic surgery in order to be more attractive or to reach the cultural standard of beauty. Most often, however, men and women report that they are getting cosmetic surgery because they want to appear normal. In general, successful plastic surgery has been shown to boost self-esteem. "The patients who are the happiest and who have had the most successful results are the ones who are properly motivated," writes Willis. "They wanted the surgery to help them feel better about themselves."[108] Those unhappy with cosmetic surgery were most often people who believed that the procedure would fix other problems in their lives.

Even as cosmetic surgery has become more common and accepted, and even as many people find it helpful, cosmetic surgery

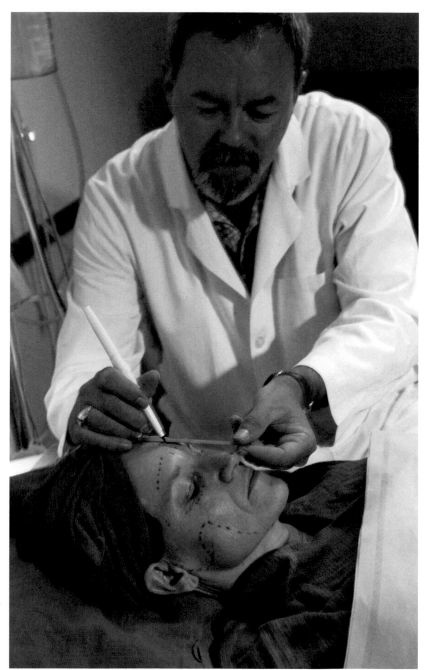

A cosmetic surgeon prepares a patient for her face lift by marking the places he will cut. Cosmetic surgery is becoming more mainstream and can even be performed at some spas.

remains controversial for safety reasons. Silicone breast implants, for instance, frequently rupture, and this can lead to serious health problems. Also, poorly performed operations by unreliable surgeons are frequently reported. In the United States, the licensing of plastic surgeons is much less stringent than other medical professions, leading to broad quality control differences between cosmetic surgery and general surgery by a doctor working under American Medical Association guidelines.

Some Americans who have undergone plastic surgery in countries where medical procedures are less regulated and much less expensive than in the United States have also had problems. Cassell and Gleaves note: "Most of the blame for this unsuccessful surgery is placed on unscrupulous and unskilled practitioners who often operate in offices with inadequate emergency equipment or inexperienced anesthetists." In some cases, the surgeries have been botched. "Most of the more than three million Americans who undergo cosmetic surgery each year are satisfied with the results, but many are mutilated."[109]

The Future

While many improvements are still necessary to make the alteration of the body safer, the advances so far achieved in plastic surgery would have been difficult to imagine fifty years ago. These processes, as Grogan has noted, have likewise offered individuals a new way of understanding their bodies. In the past, many would have accepted a number of physical features as permanent. Now, Grogan explains, body alteration offers new options. "Scientific developments in fields such as cosmetic surgery and pharmacology have given people in the Western cultures the potential to change the ways that their bodies look."[110] In offering these new options, processes like cosmetic surgery provide a way for individuals to reimagine personal identity through physical alterations.

Today, research centered on genes and DNA may eventually offer new ways of altering body images. A new philosophical movement called transhumanism imagines a future in which technology transforms bodies and minds into new forms. Russell Blackford writes: "Although there is no universally agreed definition of the word 'transhumanism,' it seems to me that the core idea is rather simple: within certain limits, it is desirable to use emerging technologies to enhance human physical and cognitive capacities, and to make other beneficial alterations to human traits."[111]

What form this might take and how it might be used to enhance body image, however, remains unknown.

While the future is always unknown, it does seem fairly certain that body image—what it means to individuals, how it is expressed socially, and how individuals choose to enhance and alter it—will remain a central and sometimes obsessive concern for both men and women.

Chapter 1: What Is Body Image?

1. *Merriam-Webster OnLine*, "Body Image," February 5, 2009.
2. National Eating Disorders Association, "Body Image," August 14, 2009. www.nationaleatingdisorders.org/p.asp?WebPage_ID=286&Profile_ID=41157.
3. Thomas Pruzinsky and Thomas F. Cash, *Body Image: A Handbook of Theory, Research, and Clinical Practice*. New York: Guilford, 2002, p. 7.
4. Barbara Moe, *Understanding the Causes of a Negative Body Image*. New York: Rosen, 1999, pp. 1–2.
5. Diane Yancey, *Eating Disorders*. Brookfield, CT: Twenty-First Century, 1999, pp. 58–59.
6. Michael P. Levine and Linda Smolak, "Body Image Development in Adolescence," in *Body Image: A Handbook of Theory and Practice*, eds. Thomas Pruzinsky and Thomas F. Cash. New York: Guilford, 2002, p. 77.
7. National Eating Disorders Association, "Body Image."
8. Joni E. Johnston, *Appearance Obsession: Learning to Love the Way We Look*. Deerfield Beach, FL: Health Communications, 1994, p. 23.
9. National Eating Disorders Association, "Body Image."
10. Rachel Huxley and YangFeng Wu, "China Too Must Confront Obesity," SciDev, August 28, 2008. www.scidev.net/en/china/opinions/china-too-must-confront-obesity.html.
11. Wang Ping, *Aching for Beauty: Footbinding in China*. New York: Anchor, 2000, p. 3.
12. Sarah Grogan, *Body Image: Understanding Body Dissatisfaction in Men, Women, and Children*. New York: Routledge, 2008, p. 16.
13. Shari Graydon, *In Your Face: The Culture of Beauty and You*. Buffalo, NY: Annick, 2004, p. 24.

14. Barbara A. Cohen, "The Psychology of Ideal Body Image as an Oppressive Force in the Lives of Women," Center for Healing the Human Spirit, 1984. www.healingthehumanspirit.com /pages/body_img.htm.

15. Bob Batchelor, *The 1900s*. Westport, CT: Greenwood, 2002, p. 92.

16. Dorothy Hoobler and Thomas Hoobler, *Vanity Rules: A History of American Fashion & Beauty*. Brookfield, CT: Twenty-First Century, 2000, p. 112.

17. Susan Brownmiller, *Femininity*. New York: Simon & Schuster, 1984, p. 47.

18. Joanna Rahim, "Interview: Sophie Dahl: 'My Granny Thinks I'm Grotesque,'" *Independent*, April 6, 1997.

19. Hillel Schwartz, *Never Satisfied: The Cultural History of Diets, Fantasies and Fat*. New York: Free Press, 1986, p. 336.

20. Gilda Marx, "The 90's Body—Toned over Thin as Ideal Body Type," *American Fitness*, January/February 1992.

Chapter 2: How Do Biology and Culture Affect Body Image?

21. Lucy Beale and Sandy G. Couvillon, "Death, Taxes, and Body Shape," FamilyEducation, 2005. http://life.familyeducation .com.

22. Emma Ross, "Genes and Biology Important in Obesity Fight," redOrbit, September 12, 2004. www.redorbit.com/news/sci ence/85683/genes_and_biology_important_in_obesity_fight.

23. Jeffrey M. Friedman, "Obesity Not a Personal Failing, but a Battle Against Biology," *Science News*, February 7, 2003. www.sciencedaily.com/releases/2003/02/030207072417.htm.

24. Johnston, *Appearance Obsession*, p. 52.

25. Linda Smolak, "Body Image Development in Children," in *Body Image: The Handbook of Theory, Research, and Clinical Practice*, eds. Thomas Pruzinsky and Thomas F. Cash. New York: Guilford, 2002, p. 69.

26. Johnston, *Appearance Obsession*, p. 53.

27. Johnston, *Appearance Obsession*, p. 52.

28. Stacey Tantleff-Dunn and Jessica L. Gokee, "Interpersonal Influences on Body Image Development," in *Body Image: The*

Handbook of Theory, Research, and Clinical Practice, eds. Thomas Pruzinsky and Thomas F. Cash. New York: Guilford, 2002, p. 110.

29. National Eating Disorders Association, "Body Image."

30. U.S. Department of Health & Human Services, "Body Image: Loving Yourself Inside and Out," March 19, 2009. www.womenshealth.gov/bodyimage.

31. Ruth H. Striegel-Moore and Debra L. Franko, "Body Image Issues Among Girls and Women," in *Body Image: The Handbook of Theory, Research, and Clinical Practice*, eds. Thomas Pruzinsky and Thomas F. Cash. New York: Guilford, 2002, p. 184.

32. Striegel-Moore and Franko, "Body Image Issues Among Girls and Women," p. 183.

33. Patricia Westmoreland Corson and Arnold E. Andersen, "Body Image Issues Among Boys and Men," in *Body Image: The Handbook of Theory, Research, and Clinical Practice*, eds. Thomas Pruzinsky and Thomas F. Cash. New York: Guilford, 2002, p. 192.

34. Smolak, "Body Image Issues Among Boys and Men," p. 194.

35. Corson and Andersen, "Body Issue Issues Among Boys and Men," p. 66.

36. Grogan, *Body Image*, pp. 150-51.

Chapter 3: Do Mass Media Distort Ideas of Body Image?

37. Jennifer L. Derenne and Eugene V. Bersin, "Body Image, Media, and Eating Disorders," *Academic Psychiatry*, May/June 2006.

38. David Croteau and William Hoynes, *Media/ Society: Industries, Images, and Societies*. Thousand Oaks, CA: Pine Forge, 2002, p. 3.

39. Kate Fox, "Mirror, Mirror," Social Issues Research Centre, 1997. www.sirc.org/publik/mirror.html.

40. Brandon Keim, "The Media Assault on the Male Body," *Seed Magazine*, September 15, 2006. http://seedmagazine.com /news/2006/09/the_media_assault_on_male_body.php.

41. Marika Tiggemann, "Media Influences on Body Image Development," in *Body Image: A Handbook of Theory and Practice*,

eds. Thomas Pruzinsky and Thomas F. Cash. New York: Guilford, 2002, p. 91.

42. Johnston, *Appearance Obsession*, p. 18.

43. Ian Halperin, *Bad and Beautiful: Inside the Dazzling and Deadly World of Supermodels*. New York: Citadel, 2001, p. 203.

44. Roxy Lee, "Body Image: Is the Media to Blame?" Roxy Lee, March 8, 2008. www.roxylee.com.

45. Johnston, *Appearance Obsession*, p. 23.

46. Quoted in Spliced Wire, "All America(n) Girl," September 18, 2002. www.splicedwire.com/02features/aferrera.html.

47. Quoted in Alan Freeman, "Diet by Airbrush: Magazine Creates a Leaner Kate Winslet," *Globe and Mail*, January 16, 2003. http://archive.southcoasttoday.com/daily/01-03/01-16-03/c20li152.htm.

48. Dove, "Self-Esteem Is Worth Sharing," September 2008. www.dove.us/#/CFRB/selfesteem.

49. Buggheart, "The Mag for Plus Size Women Is Not Meaty Enough," Viewpoints, August 2008. www.viewpoints.com /Figure-Magazine-review-3af44.

Chapter 4: Does Advertising Distort Body Image?

50. Shari Graydon, *Made You Look: How Advertising Works and Why You Should Know*. Buffalo, NY: Annick, 2003, p. 1.

51. Allen Teal, "How Advertising Affects Body Images," Socyberty, January 20, 2008. http://socyberty.com/society/how-adver tising-affects-body-image.

52. Quoted in Bryan Holme, *Advertising, Reflections of a Century*. New York: Viking, 1982, p. 18.

53. Quoted in Holme, *Advertising, Reflections of a Century*, p. 268.

54. Alissa Quart, *Branded: The Buying and Selling of Teenagers*. New York: Perseus, 2003, p. xvi.

55. Media Awareness Network, "Special Issues for Tweens and Teens: The 'Tween Market,'" August 2009. www.media-awareness.ca./english/parents/marketing/issues_teens_mar keting.cfm.

56. James Sullivan, *Jeans: A Cultural History of An American Icon*. New York: Gotham, 2006, p. 177.

57. Sullivan, *Jeans*, p. 166.

58. Tom Reichert and Jacqueline Lambiase, eds., *Sex in Advertising: Perspectives on the Erotic Appeal*. Mahwah, NJ: Lawrence Erlbaum, 2003, p. 60.

59. Pamela A. Ivinski, "I See London, I See France, I See Calvin's Underpants," in *Sex Appeal: The Art of Allure in Graphic and Advertising Design*, ed. Steven Heller. New York: Allworth, 2000, p. 115.

60. Michelle Lee, *Fashion Victim: Our Love-Hate Relationship with Dressing, Shopping, and the Cost of Style*. New York: Broadway, 2003, p. 46.

61. Media Awareness Network, "Beauty and Body Image in the Media," 2008. www.media-awareness.ca/english/issues/stereo typing/women_and_girls/women_beauty.cfm.

62. Halperin, *Bad and Beautiful*, p. 203.

63. Grogan, *Body Image*, pp. 108–109.

64. Shari Graydon, *Made You Look: How Advertising Works and Why You Should Know*. New York: Annick, 2003, p. 65.

65. Quart, *Branded*, p. 116.

Chapter 5: Body Image and Obsession

66. Johnston, *Appearance Obsession*, pp. 17–18.

67. Fox, "Mirror, Mirror."

68. Johnston, *Appearance Obsession*, p. 24.

69. H.W. Hoek and D. van Hoeken, "Review of the Prevalence and Incidence of Eating Disorders," *International Journal of Eating Disorders*, 2003, pp. 383–96.

70. World Health Organization, "Obesity and Overweight," January 2010. www.who.int/dietphysicalactivity/publications/facts/obesity/en.

71. Quoted in Columbia University Mailman School of Public Health, "Body Image Is a Stronger Predictor of Health than Obesity, According to Mailman School of Public Health Study," February 28, 2008. http://mailman.hs.columbia.edu/news/article?article=617.

72. Peter N. Stearns, *Fat History: Bodies and Beauty in the Modern West*. New York: New York University, 1997, p. 247.

73. BBC, "Many People Diet Most of the Time," February 4, 2004. http://news.bbc.co.uk/1/hi/health/3454099.stm.

74. Rebecca Reisner, "The Diet Industry: A Big Fat Lie," *BusinessWeek*, February 2, 2009. www.businessweek.com/debateroom/archives/2008/01/the_diet_indust.html.

75. Dana K. Cassell and David H. Gleaves, *The Encyclopedia of Obesity and Eating Disorders*. New York: Facts On File, 2000, p. 91.

76. Kathy Kater, "Body Image Blues," eNotAlone, 2004. www.enotalone.com/article/4351.html.

77. Cassell and Gleaves, *The Encyclopedia of Obesity and Eating Disorders*, p. 53.

78. Joan Jacobs Brumberg, *Fasting Girls: The History of Anorexia Nervosa*, rev. ed. New York: Vintage, 2000, p. 15.

79. Helpguide.org, "Anorexia Nervosa," August 2009. http://helpguide.org/mental/anorexia_signs_symptoms_causes_treatment.htm.

80. Yancey, *Eating Disorders*, p. 24.

81. Yancey, *Eating Disorders*, p. 24.

82. Yancey, *Eating Disorders*, p. 24.

83. Michelle Biton, "Are You Exercise Obsessed?" *alive*, February 1, 2009. www.alive.com/1482a4a2.php?subject_bread_cramb=6.

84. Cassell and Gleaves, *The Encyclopedia of Obesity and Eating Disorders*, p. 88.

85. Grogan, *Body Image*, p. 95.

86. Grogan, *Body Image*, p. 63.

87. Mayo Clinic, "Body Dysmorphic Disorder," February 2, 2009. www.mayoclinic.com/health/body-dysmorphic-disorder/DS00559/DSECTION=symptoms.

88. Harrison G. Pope Jr., Katherine A. Phillips, and Roberto Olivardia, "A Health Crisis That Strikes Men of All Ages," eNot Alone, 2000. www.enotalone.com/article/5532.html.

89. David Batty, "Men and Body Image: Do You Have an Adonis Complex?" Net Doctor, February 2, 2009. www.netdoctor.co.uk/menshealth/feature/adonis.htm.

90. P/S/L Group, "Doctor's Guide: Muscle Dysmorphia—Bodybuilding Gone Amuck," February 2, 2009. www.pslgroup.com/dg/47BFE.htm.

Chapter 6: Altering Body Image

91. Graydon, *In Your Face*, p. 45.
92. Julian Robinson, *The Quest for Human Beauty: An Illustrated Guide*. New York: Norton, 1998, p. 81.
93. Grogan, *Body Image*, p. 36.
94. KidsHealth, "Body Piercing," February 2, 2009. http://kids health.org/teen/your_body/skin_stuff/body_piercing_safe .html.
95. Robinson, *The Quest for Human Beauty*, p. 197.
96. Grogan, *Body Image*, p. 40.
97. Arthur W. Perry, *Straight Talk About Cosmetic Surgery*. New Haven, CT: Yale University Press, 2007, p. 221.
98. Grogan, *Body Image*, p. 40.
99. Richard Backstein and Anna Hinek, "War and Medicine: The Origins of Plastic Surgery," *UTMG*, May 2005, p. 218. www.utmj.org/issues/82.3/Historical_Review__82-3-217.pdf.
100. Perry, *Straight Talk About Cosmetic Surgery*, p. 3.
101. Perry, *Straight Talk About Cosmetic Surgery*, p. 3.
102. Jan Willis, *Beautiful Again: Restoring Your Image & Enhancing Body Changes*. Santa Fe, NM: Health Press, 1994, p. 167.
103. Graydon, *In Your Face*, p. 59.
104. Backstein and Hinek, "War and Medicine," p. 219.
105. Perry, *Straight Talk About Cosmetic Surgery*, p. 7.
106. American Society of Aesthetic Plastic Surgery, "Quick Facts," January 2010. www.surgery.org/media/statistics.
107. Grogan, *Body Image*, p. 40.
108. Willis, *Beautiful Again*, p. 167.
109. Cassell and Gleaves, *The Encyclopedia of Obesity and Eating Disorders*, p. 63.
110. Grogan, *Body Image*, p. 206.
111. Russell Blackford, "The Core Idea of Transhumanism," Sentient Developments, January 22, 2009. www.sentientdevel opments.com/2009/01/guest-blogger-russell-blackford-on.html.

DISCUSSION QUESTIONS

Chapter 1: What Is Body Image?

1. How does the author define body image?
2. How has the ideal body type changed over time?
3. What is the difference between positive and negative body image?

Chapter 2: How Do Biology and Culture Affect Body Image?

1. How is the development of body image affected by biology?
2. In what ways do family and peers affect body image?
3. Does gender influence the development of body image issues?
4. How are body image concerns different for children, adolescents, and adults?

Chapter 3: Do Mass Media Distort Ideas of Body Image?

1. Do mass media offer a realistic ideal of body types?
2. What do the media represent to be the ideal male body type?
3. What do the media represent to be the ideal female body type?
4. How have the media changed its presentation of body types because of criticism?

Chapter 4: Does Advertising Distort Body Image?

1. Is the use of body image in advertising a contemporary phenomenon?
2. Are models naturally thin and attractive, or does working as a model require a great deal of effort to achieve the perfect look?
3. Can you give an example of how advertisers have used sexuality to sell a product?

Chapter 5: Body Image and Obsession

1. Why does author Joni. E. Johnston believe that concern with body image has become an obsession?

2. What are the most common eating disorders? What do they share in common and how are they different?

3. How does the use of anabolic steroids affect men and women?

Chapter 6: Altering Body Image

1. How have mainstream attitudes changed in relation to tattoos, body piercing, and cosmetic surgery?

2. What are the differences and similarities between reconstructive and cosmetic surgery?

3. What motivates most people to seek out cosmetic surgery?

ORGANIZATIONS TO CONTACT

American Academy of Child and Adolescent Psychiatry (AACAP)
3615 Wisconsin Ave. NW
Washington, DC 20016-3007
phone: (202) 966-7300
fax: (202) 966-2891
Web site: www.aacap.org

AACAP is a nonprofit organization dedicated to providing parents and families with information regarding developmental, behavioral, and mental disorders that affect children and adolescents. The organization provides national public information through the distribution of the newsletter *Facts for Families* and the monthly *Journal of the American Academy of Child and Adolescent Psychiatry*.

Commercial Alert
PO Box 19002
Washington, DC 20036
phone: (202) 387-8030
fax: (202) 234-5176
e-mail: jennifer@commercialalert.org
Web site: www.commercialalert.org

Commercial Alert is a nonprofit organization whose goal is to prevent commercial culture from exploiting children and destroying family and community values. It works toward that goal by conducting campaigns against commercialism in classrooms and marketing to children. News and opportunities to take action against various marketing tactics are posted on the Web site.

KidsHealth.org
PO Box 269
Wilmington, DE 19899

e-mail: webmaster@KidsHealth.org
Web site: www.kidshealth.org/kid/

KidsHealth is a Web site providing doctor-approved health information about children from before birth through adolescence. Created by the Nemours Foundation's Center for Children's Health Media, KidsHealth provides families with accurate, up-to-date, and jargon-free health information they can use. KidsHealth has been on the Web since 1995.

Mayo Health Clinic
200 First St. SW
Rochester, MN 55905
phone: (507) 284-2511
Web site: www.mayoclinic.com

The Mayo Clinic is a not-for-profit medical practice devoted to the diagnosis and treatment of virtually every type of complex illness. Doctors, specialists, and other health care professionals provide comprehensive diagnosis, understandable answers, and effective treatment. The Mayo Clinic has sites in Rochester, Minnesota; Jacksonville, Florida; and Scottsdale-Phoenix area in Arizona. Collectively, the three locations treat more than half a million people each year.

National Association of Anorexia and Associated Disorders (ANAD)
Box 7
Highland Park, IL 60035
phone: (847) 831-3438
fax: (847) 433-4632
e-mail: anad20@aol.com
Web site: http://members.aol.com/anad20

ANAD offers hot-line counseling, operates an international network of support groups for people with eating disorders and their families, and provides referrals to health care professionals who treat eating disorders. It produces a quarterly newsletter and information packets and organizes national conferences and local programs. All ANAD services are provided free of charge.

Society for Adolescent Medicine (SAM)
1916 NW Copper Oaks Circle
Blue Springs, MO 64015
phone: (816) 224-8010
Web site: www.adolescenthealth.org

SAM is a multidisciplinary organization of professionals committed to improving the physical and psychosocial health and well-being of all adolescents. It helps plan and coordinate national and international professional education programs on adolescent health. Its publications include the monthly *Journal of Adolescent Health* and the quarterly *SAM Newsletter*.

FOR MORE INFORMATION

Books and Periodicals

Joan Jacobs Brumberg, *The Body Project: An Intimate History of American Girls*. New York: Vintage, 1998. This book details the dramatic changes that American girls and women have experienced in relationship to body image issues from the Victorian era until the 1990s.

Thomas Cash, *The Body Image Workbook: An Eight-Step Program for Learning to Like Your Looks*. Oakland, CA: New Harbinger, 2008. This instruction book offers practical advice on understanding body image issues along with a method for working through personal issues focused on body image in a positive manner.

Shari Graydon, *In Your Face: The Culture of Beauty and You*. Buffalo, NY: Annick, 2004. The author provides an overview of the beauty culture and how it impacts the behavior of men and women.

Shari Graydon, *Made You Look: How Advertising Works and Why You Should Know*. Buffalo, NY: Annick, 2003. An inside look at the advertising industry and the methods it uses to attract consumers.

Shari Graydon, *Body Image: Understanding Body Dissatisfaction in Men, Women, and Children*. New York: Routledge, 2007. The author uses multiple studies to offer an in-depth analysis of body image issues.

Ian Halperin, *Bad and Beautiful: Inside the Dazzling and Deadly World of Supermodels*. New York: Citadel, 2001. A critical overview of the fashion industry and an intimate look at the lives of supermodels.

Alissa Quart, *Branded: The Buying and Selling of Teenagers*. New York: Perseus, 2003. The author argues that advertisers use dishonest methods to persuade teenagers of the importance of brand names.

Nancy Amanda Redd, *Body Drama: Real Girls, Real Bodies, Real Issues, Real Answers*. New York: Gotham, 2007. The author offers an exploration of a number of body image issues experienced by young women, offering fresh perspectives on ideas of beauty and debunking common myths about differences in body types.

Rebecca Reisner and Derek Thompson, "The Diet Industry: A Big Fat Lie," *BusinessWeek*, February 2, 2009. www.business week.com/debateroom/archives/2008/01/the_diet_indust.html. Reisner and Thompson offer two sides to whether or not diets work, with Reisner blaming the industry for false advertising and Thompson blaming consumers for believing in easy solutions.

David Veale, Robert Wilson, and Alex Clarke, *Overcoming Body Image Problems Including Body Dysmorphic Disorder: A Self-Help Guide Using Cognitive Behavioral Techniques*. New York: Basic Books, 2009. Part of the *Overcoming* series, this book offers a number of practical methods for overcoming a variety of body image disorders.

Web Sites

Adios Barbie (www.adiosbarbie.com). Adios Barbie strives to support a broad community in building a healthy body and self image. This includes recognition of cultural and size differences in body image considerations, and the organization promotes the acceptance of these differences. The Web site addresses media influences and includes links to multiple resources for eating disorders.

Media Awareness Network (www.media-awareness.ca). Media Awareness Network is a Canadian nonprofit organization that promotes media literacy. The organization provides online programs, resources, and educational games. The Media Awareness Network also focuses on how the media portray body image and beauty.

National Eating Disorders Association (NEDA) (www.na tionaleatingdisorders.org). The NEDA provides education and resources for those affected by eating disorders. The organization campaigns for increased funding for research and treatment related to eating disorders. The NEDA also serves as a clearinghouse for information on eating disorders and partners with various organizations to facilitate this purpose.

National Institute of Mental Health (NIMH) (www.nimh .nih.gov/index.shtml). The NIMH focuses on a broad variety of mental health issues including eating disorders. The organization issues multiple publications, including *Eating Disorders*, 2008, and issues research grants in a variety of scientific fields.

Our Bodies Ourselves (www.ourbodiesourselves.org). The Boston Women's Health Book Collective (BWHBC) is a nonprofit organization that first published *Our Bodies, Ourselves* in 1970. The organization continues to support educational efforts related to women's health issues, including maintaining a Web site dedicated to the free distribution of information.

Something Fishy (www.something-fishy.org/reach/bodyimage .php). Something Fishy offers information on a wide variety of eating disorders. The Web site includes questionnaires, fact sheets, and information on seeking treatment for eating disorders.

Teens Health (http://kidshealth.org/teen). Teens Health provides educational information and advice for teenagers. The organization is nonprofit and includes a qualified staff of health professionals. Articles cover multiple body image issues from self-esteem to body piercings.

INDEX

PICTURE CREDITS

Cover: Image copyright Phil Date, 2009. Used under license from Shutterstock.com
AP Images, 41, 49, 59, 90
© Bettmann/Corbis, 19
Brent Stirton/Reportage/Getty Images, 87
© Bubbles Photolibrary/Alamy, 29, 73
© Carl and Ann Purcell/Corbis, 52
© Chris Rout/Alamy, 40
© Corbis, 20
© David J. Green - lifestyle themes/Alamy, 31
© Dennis Galante/Corbis, 69
Ethan Miller/Getty Images, 53
Image copyright Gabriel Moisa, 2009. Used under license from Shutterstock.com, 76
Image copyright Glenda M. Powers, 2009. Used under license from Shutterstock.com, 34
© Jim Cornfield/Corbis, 8
© keith morris/Alamy, 7
© Leonard Lessin, FBPA/Photo Researchers, Inc., 24
Image copyright Lisa F. Young, 2009. Used under license from Shutterstock.com, 26, 36
© Mary Evans Picture Library/Alamy, 17
© Matthew Totton/Alamy, 83
© Michael Paul/Bon Appetit/Alamy, 66
© Michelle Del Guercio/Photo Researchers, Inc., 80
© Phototake Inc/Alamy, 12
© Richard G. Bingham II/Alamy, 39
© Richard Levine/Alamy, 56
Steve Zmina/Gale, Cengage Learning, 30, 68
© Susan McCartney/Photo Researchers, Inc., 81
The Kobal Collection, 47

ABOUT THE AUTHOR

Ronald D. Lankford Jr. is a freelance writer and independent scholar. His first book, *Folk Music USA*, was a popular history of the American Folk Revival (1958–1965), published in 2005. His most recent book, *Women Singer-Songwriters in Rock: A Populist Rebellion in the 1990s*, was published by Scarecrow Press in 2010. He has edited a number of titles for Greenhaven Press, including *Can Diets Be Harmful? Is American Society Too Materialistic?* and *Polygamy*. He currently resides with his wife Elizabeth and seven cats in Appomattox, Virginia.

	DATE DUE		